THE PAVEMENT OF HELL

The Pavement of Hell

LEONARD TUSHNET

ST. MARTIN'S PRESS   NEW YORK

ST. MARTIN'S PRESS   NEW YORK

St. Martin's Press
175 Fifth Avenue
New York, N.Y. 10010

Affiliated Publishers:
Macmillan & Company, Limited, London
—also at Bombay, Calcutta, Madras and Melbourne—

FOR MY WIFE, FANNIE

אֵשֶׁת חַיִל מִי יִמְצָא וְרָחֹק מִפְּנִינִים מִכְרָהּ

(Proverbs 31:10)

Acknowledgments

No book on the events of the Holocaust can be written without paying tribute to the dozens of men, women, and children (yes, children!) who left notes, diaries, and accounts of the times they died in, and to those survivors who recorded the horrors of the period. They are not forgotten.

My deepest gratitude goes to the staff of YIVO-Institute for Jewish Research, especially to Miss Dina Abramowicz, librarian, and Mr. Ezekiel Lifschutz, its former archivist, for their attention and interest, and to Dr. Isaiah Trunk, who read a portion of the manuscript and gave me many helpful suggestions.

The staff of the Jewish Room at the New York Public Library and the staff of the Maplewood, New Jersey, Public Library both have my thanks for their patience with me.

I received tremendous assistance from Mrs. Jacob Gens and Mrs. Ada Ustjanauskas, who overcame painful memories in order to give me information about Jacob Gens. Many obscure details would have remained obscure had it not been for their help.

Others who cooperated with me in my research include Dr.

Samuel Schulsinger, Mr.Walter Ackerman, Mr. Joseph Green-blatt, Mr. Yuri Suhl, Mr. Arie Ben-Sholom, Mr. Jack Moss, Mr. Anicetas Simutis, Consul-General of Lithuania, and Mr. E. Yushkis, Consular Secretary of the Embassy of the USSR. My heartfelt thanks to them all.

Needless to say, none of those I have mentioned have any responsibility for the viewpoints expressed in this book. For those I alone am accountable.

Foreword

The heart's intention is the measure of all things.
Maimonides, *Guide to the Perplexed*

So much has been made of the villainy of the leaders of the Jewish
Councils in Nazi-occupied Europe that the very name "Judenrat"
has taken on pejorative overtones. The contemporary literature
of the Holocaust teems with execrations against them as exem-
plars of the basest of creatures, as traitors to their people, as vic-
ious and vile lackeys of their German overlords. Later analyses
of Jewish life under the Nazis built on those characterizations
ingenious psychological theories about the genocide of the Jews,
equating the murderers with their victims and the guiltless with
the guilty. It is time now to look soberly (not dispassionately—no
one can be dispassionate before the terrible truth) at the facts,
at the circumstances and the actions of those Jews who were in
a position of leadership.

Who were those heads of the Jewish Councils? Who made them
leaders? Were they, as has been said time and again, bellwethers

leading their followers to destruction? Were they self-servers willing to sacrifice others for their own personal gain or safety? Or were they stupid, and paid in the wages of stupidity, which is death? Or did they deliberately blind themselves to what was happening to the Jews under their control?

To answer such questions requires examination of their lives and avowed motivations. Since every man is not like other men, volumes would be needed to describe all the leaders. And yet I believe there were similarities, and from those similarities shown in the roles particular men played in the events of that time, some generalizations can be made. In that belief I have confined myself to the terminal biographies of three men, all leaders of ghettos in Eastern Europe and all differing in their backgrounds and philosophies. The three are Adam Czerniakow of Warsaw, Mordecai Chaim Rumkowski of Lodz, and Jacob Gens of Vilna.

Probably because of the heroic resistance that developed in the days of the destruction of the Warsaw Ghetto, general descriptions of that ghetto abound in works accessible to readers of English. That is not true of the Ghetto of Lodz, and less so of the Ghetto of Vilna.

The largest ghetto in Europe was that of Warsaw, part of the *General-Gouvernement,* the name the Germans gave to that part of Poland treated as a conquered province. The Warsaw Ghetto was surrounded by a high brick wall, but it was in a part of an urban area whose Polish inhabitants were not all inimical to the Jews; movement in and out of the ghetto required official permission, and unofficial movement was difficult and dangerous but not impossible; once beyond the wall, "passing as an Aryan" was feasible; in the countryside nearby were hiding places and a few partisan outposts.

The Lodz Ghetto belonged to the Wartheland, a section of Poland that was integrated into the Third Reich; it was ringed only by barbed wire and a board fence but was nevertheless more hermetically sealed off than the walled Warsaw Ghetto. In spite of the open fields beyond it, escape would be only into the hands of the Germans and *Volksdeutsche* (ethnic Germans) who lived in the adjoining city and the surrounding farms.

The Vilna Ghetto was established in what had been Polish territory, then independent Lithuania, and then a Soviet Republic. Much smaller than the Ghettos of Warsaw and Lodz, it had a gate, but there was ready access to the rest of the city; indeed, it was in the center of the city. Movement to and from the nearby forests took place; an organized and armed resistance group existed; the attitude of the indigenous Poles and Lithuanians ranged from cooperation to indifference to rabid anti-Semitism.

Adam Czerniakow was the Chairman of the Warsaw Judenrat (Jewish Council). Mordecai Chaim Rumkowski was "the Eldest of the Jews" in Lodz. Jacob Gens was the Chief of the Vilna Ghetto.

Tragedy in art gives understanding of man's strivings and failings as well as catharsis. We know what will happen to Oedipus and yet we follow the play with mounting terror as the inexorable workings of his destiny unfold. We try to comprehend what strengths and what weaknesses brought him to his blind end. Putting aside all prejudice, we should seek to understand why Rumkowski, Czerniakow, and Gens did what they did. Their deeds arose, not from decrees of the gods, but from a carefully considered rationality that was, alas! to bear bitter consequences. I believe the stories of their lives will confirm the conclusion expressed in the title of this book: that they were men who had good intentions. Their feet laid hold on Hell, but the paths that led to the death camps of Chelmno, Treblinka, Majdanek, and Auschwitz were not of their making.

King Chaim

Dr. Emanuel Ringelblum, the founder of the secret archives of the Warsaw Ghetto, wrote in his notes on September 6, 1940:

> Today . . . there arrived from Lodz, Chaim, or as he is called, "King Chaim" Rumkowski, an old man of seventy years, extraordinarily ambitious and a little nutty. He recited the marvels of the ghetto. He has a Jewish kingdom there, with four hundred policemen, three jails. He has a foreign ministry, as well as all the other ministries. When asked why, if things are so good there, the mortality is so high, he did not answer. He considers himself God's anointed.

1

The Germans overran Poland in September, 1939, and promptly divided it into several administrative districts. Much of western Poland became integrated into the Reich under the name of the Wartheland.

Lodz, known for its textile industries, was the second largest city in Poland. It was also the second largest Jewish center (after Warsaw) in all of Europe, with a Jewish community of 233,000, making up a third of the city's population. The Nazis renamed the city Litzmannstadt in honor of Litzmann, the German general who had captured it in the First World War. The German geopoliticians planned that Litzmannstadt, like the rest of the Wartheland, was to become wholly German. Many of the Poles in the city and surrounding farmlands were forced to leave. They were replaced by Germans from the west, rewarded for being born into the Master Race, by Volksdeutsche—ethnic Germans who had been living in Poland for generations, and by Germans who left the new Baltic Soviet Republics.

Lodz was occupied on September 8, 1939. Immediately there began a period of terror, beatings, looting, and murder of the Jews. Poles, Volksdeutsche, and German soldiers all joined in the fun. The military authorities made no attempt to restrain the attacks, busy as they were with the conquest of Poland. The Gestapo and SS men who came with the army were also busy seeking out for arrest the leaders of the Polish and Jewish intelligentsia, the heads of the labor unions, and the activists in the political parties; they had a prepared list furnished by the Fifth Column of Volksdeutsche in Lodz.

Most of the Polish and Jewish notables had fled before the German advance to the safety of Bialystok and Vilna, soon to come under Soviet rule. Among the refugees was Leibel Mintzberg, the president of the *Kehillah* (Jewish Community Council), a semiautonomous official body elected by the Jewish population of Lodz. The Kehillah dealt with specifically Jewish matters: the organization and support of Jewish schools, the maintenance of Jewish hospitals and other philanthropic institutions, the licensing of ritual slaughterers, etc. Mintzberg's place was taken by Leiser I. Plivatski, the vice-president, and a new vice-president was chosen, Mordecai Chaim Rumkowski.

2

Mordecai Chaim Rumkowski was born in Vilna, Lithuania

(then part of the Russian Empire), on March 17, 1877, to a poor workingman. His early life was beset by privation. His education was limited: he attended a *Cheder* taught by a bored and impatient teacher, where he learned to read and write Hebrew and was introduced to formal religion. For a very short time he also attended a Russian primary school. His native tongue was a Yiddish dialect, but he quickly learned Russian and Polish.

Lodz, with its rapidly growing textile industry, in the closing years of the nineteenth century was a magnet that drew to it hundreds of ambitious young men, energetic and willing, eager to make their fortunes. Rumkowski was one of those young men seeking a way out of the miseries of the Jewish Pale of Settlement. He had great drive and a greater confidence in his ability. Unlike so many of his contemporaries, he was not discouraged by the intense competition but in true Horatio Alger fashion made his way up in the world to become eventually a partner in a factory that made silk and plush fabrics. With his success went philanthropy; he was a generous donor to Jewish communal institutions, especially those concerned with children. Unfortunately, after a series of business reverses his firm went bankrupt. Rumkowski felt the bankruptcy was a reflection on his honor. Although he knew not a word of English, he left for England to try to come to an agreement with his creditors; he wanted to pay off his debts to them and get their support for further ventures.

He was successful. He impressed the English financiers and got enough money to start in business again, this time as a textile manufacturer in Russia proper. Business boomed for him. He was once more on the way to wealth, but the outbreak of World War I and the Russian Revolution put an end to his hopes. He lost almost his entire fortune. He returned to Lodz to start again, poor, a widower twice over, childless.

Few opportunities existed in the textile trades in postwar, newly independent Poland. Rumkowski became an insurance agent. He diverted his energy and ambition to Jewish communal affairs, with a particular interest in orphaned children. In 1920 the

American Joint Distribution Committee sent a large sum of money to Lodz to set up summer camps for children. The Kehillah chose three men to supervise the camps: Solomon I. Ravin, Abraham Kagan, and Rumkowski. The first two were members of the Bundist (Jewish-socialist) and Zionist intelligentsia. Rumkowski was chosen because of his integrity, his special solicitude for orphans, and his enthusiastic efforts for their care.

Rumkowski was zealous in his labors. He became known as "the Father of the Orphans." His endeavors for them led to his appointment as general supervisor of several orphan asylums in Lodz. An indefatigable fund-raiser, he used his past connections with local manufacturers to get them to support openhandedly his orphan asylums. One of them, Pincus Gershowski, gave him the magnificent sum of 300,000 zlotys. With the money, Rumkowski constructed in the Lodz suburbs a modern orphan asylum with three large buildings. This institution had the reputation of being the best in Poland. Rumkowski wanted to make it even better. He went to Dr. Janusz Korczak, the pediatrician famous for his theories of child education, to study his methods of pedagogy, and he introduced many progressive techniques into the asylum. He wanted to spread the gospel of Korczak's methods. For several years he published a journal, *The Orphan*, whose editor was Dr. Langeleben, a member of the Orthodox Party. Attached to the orphan asylum was a special school for agricultural work to train young people to be farmers and encourage them to emigrate to Palestine.

The latter project was consistent with his Zionist views. Rumkowski was then a member of the General Zionist Party, the centrist division of the Zionist movement. Zionism, the expression of hope for a Jewish homeland, had been for years steadily gaining adherents in world Jewry. The Jews, especially those of Europe with memories of the Dreyfus case, blood libels, and pogroms, saw in the Holy Land, their historic birthplace, a refuge from persecution and a country where the ideas of Isaiah and the prophets or of Moses Hess, Theodor Herzl, and Karl Marx could be developed so that the Jews would once again be a light unto the

Gentiles. Two strands thus were woven into the fabric of Zionism: the religious hope for the ingathering that would presage the coming of the Messiah and the unbelievers' hope for a socialist utopia. As the Zionist movement grew, so did the tension between the two ideologies. The General Zionist branch of the movement arose early in the 1900's as a compromise and as an expression of those Jews who wanted a homeland but who were neither religious nor socialist. The General Zionists said that Jews in the Diaspora should favor no special group but that they should work in the interests of Jewish settlements in Palestine. They felt that Zionism stood above class and factional struggle, that labor and capital must unite to build a Jewish state, and that private investment and enterprise should be encouraged, not frowned upon.

Zionism was by no means heartily endorsed by Polish Jews. Strict Orthodox Jews regarded it as an attempt to force the hand of the Almighty. Hardheaded businessmen and the socialist Bundists alike saw Zionism as a visionary, sentimental answer to the pressing problems of the Jews in Poland; both looked to internationalism in the form of enlightened capitalism or of socialism to do away with the persecution of the Jews. The capitalists feared that Zionism was a weapon handed to the native anti-Semites, a proof of the divided loyalties of the Jews. The socialists saw in Zionism a bourgeois diversionary tactic to obscure the class struggle.

Rumkowski was an enthusiastic Zionist. He never hesitated to make propaganda for the cause. In spite of his patent zeal, however, he was looked down on by the professional Zionists because of his lack of formal education. He was never considered for any post of importance. He was elected to the Kehillah, the administrative body for Jewish affairs, it is true, but at the very bottom of the Zionist list; his later post in the Kehillah executive was ex-officio as director of the new orphan asylum. Rumkowski's skin was thick enough to withstand the slights of his fellow-workers in the Kehillah. He was aggressive and vocal, never hesitating to fight for his two pet projects: his orphan asylum and the Jewish National Fund to buy land in Palestine. If he felt that either was being discriminated against in the allotment of communal funds, he disrupted the meeting by his demands to be heard; once given the floor, he would not yield it but would speak for hours until his opponents gave up out of sheer weariness. His "folkishness," the direct and artless way he pressed forward and expressed his opinions, brought him many supporters in the Jewish community. He soon became recognized as an important leader of the Zionists againt the *Agudah* (Orthodox majority in the Kehillah.)

He ruled the orphan asylum with an iron hand and made enemies in the staff by his arbitrariness. A teacher whom he dismissed accused him of committing immoral acts with female orphans. The charges were unproved (indeed, they were never investigated), but the mere fact that they had been made caused the Zionist functionaries, already prejudiced against him because of his lack of education, to further distrust him on the grounds that Caesar's wife must be above suspicion.

They had other reasons for distrust. By the middle 1930's Rumkowski had begun, with the support of the (Jewish) Craftsmen's Alliance, a movement toward a policy of accommodation with the Polish government. Official anti-Semitism was then on the increase; discriminatory laws against Jews were being passed. Influential Jewish leaders, mainly among the Orthodox, had decided to submit and work with the regime while they tried to mitigate the severity of the discriminatory laws by evasion, bribery, and the other methods so successfully used by the Jews under Tsarist rule. The Zionists refused to cooperate in any way with the government. Rumkowski said they were wrong: Hitler was already in power in Germany; anti-Semitic as the Polish regime was, it was still better than Nazi rule, an ever-increasing danger. Rumkowski became a fiery Polish patriot. The conflict in the Kehillah over the accommodation policy increased. When the Agudah majority voted down the Zionist resolutions to subsidize Zionist funds and institutions, the Zionists withdrew en masse. Not Rumkowski. He was expelled from the General Zionist Party for violation of party discipline, but he shrugged off the expulsion. Why should he leave the Kehillah, he reasoned, and give up the only post of honor he ever had in the Jewish community just to stay with a bunch of wrong-headed people who had no use for him? With the same energy he had previously displayed for the Zionists he now worked with the Agudah majority to further the policy of accommodation.

He was not the only Zionist who felt that the Orthodox were right. The increasing distress of the workers under the anti-Semitic laws led many to believe that giving up their anti-government stand might improve their lot. They recognized Rumkowski as their spokesman. He had further endeared himself to them by refusing, although he still ran an insurance agency, to write any insurance policies for the properties owned by the Kehillah lest he be accused of a conflict of interests and of profiting by his communal position. Such an upright attitude was incomprehensible to his bourgeois colleagues on the Kehillah to whom "business was business." The workers, however, saw in Rumkowski's stand proof of his integrity. He had enough support to be readmitted to the General Zionist Party in April, 1939, and to be placed on their list of candidates for the Kehillah. He was reelected.

After the German occupation, his selection as vice-president of the Kehillah filled him with joy. Enthusiastic and ambitious, he felt that the time had come for him to show the Jewish community what kind of a man he was, how he could serve his people as no other communal activist ever had, particularly in a time of troubles.

3

A month after the occupation, on October 8, 1939, German law superseded Polish law in Litzmannstadt; representative government gave way, as in the rest of the Reich, to the leadership principle; order replaced the disorder of war. Acts of hooliganism against the Jews gradually decreased. The Germans had plans to solve the Jewish question more systematically than by beatings.

The Kehillah began falteringly to take up its prewar functions —plus a new one. Jews were being seized daily on the streets and in their homes to be taken away for forced labor at road building, airfield construction, and the removal of debris. The forced labor was actually slavery, under conditions that frequently led to the death of the laborers. To ease the terror aroused by such seizures, the Kehillah proposed to the Germans that it would supply a daily contingent of workers. A census of unemployed Jewish workers was taken; an office for supplying the Germans with a labor force was set up. The street seizures, with a few exceptions, stopped. A resigned yet hopeful attitude began to appear among the Jews. "We survived other troubles, we'll survive this one," was the common saying. Stores and businesses began to reopen. The Kehillah started plans for an orderly existence.

On October 14, 1939, the Germans summoned a meeting of the Kehillah. There the members were notified that all Jewish cultural and social organizations, including the Kehillah, were dissolved. Impressed by Rumkowski's dignified appearance (he was erect, clean-shaven, with piercing blue eyes and a silvery head of hair), the German city commissioner appointed him as "the Eldest of the Jews" and ordered him to set up an advisory Council of Elders. The title followed from the German belief in their own propaganda that a secret council of elders ruled over the Jews; if so, then the leader of that council must necessarily be "the Eldest." Rumkowski was given full authority over all those "who belonged to the Jewish race" to see that the directives of the German administration were carried out. He was made personally responsible to the city commissioner for the execution of all orders. By virtue of his office he was exempted from the curfew regulations; he was permitted to wear a special insigne, to enter German offices on business, to organize requisitions, and to control the forced labor centers. All Jews were ordered to obey Rumkowski's instructions under penalty of punishment by the Germans. Every Jewish institution was to be reorganized under his control in accordance with the leadership principle.

On the previous day, however, another German official, taking it for granted that rabbis ruled over the Jews, had ordered Rabbi S. Treistman, a graduate of a Berlin seminary, the secretary of the Lodz rabbinate, to arrange for the continuance and enlargement of the labor gangs. Rumkowski was annoyed by such a division of authority. He ignored Rabbi Treistman's suggestions. He "forgot" to pay him the stipend he was entitled to as an ordained rabbi. In general he made life so miserable for the rabbi that the latter, a couple of months later, fled from Lodz in disgust and made his way to Warsaw.

The Council of Elders was not elected by the community, as the Kehillah had been. It was formed arbitrarily by Rumkowski himself from a list he drew up of Jewish leaders present in the city. He sent notices to the thirty he chose in the following words (in Polish), "Following the order of the City Commissioner of Lodz, you are appointed to the Council of Elders of the Jewish religious community of Lodz. Acceptance of this nomination is compulsory." Rumkowski looked to the Council for advice on how to reorganize Jewish life, but he made it clear that he wanted only advice. He was the executive; he alone would have the final decision on what to do and how to do it. Rumkowski's ambition and the German führer-principle were perfectly congruent.

But Rumkowski's ambition was not that of the simple seeker after glory for glory's sake. He wanted honor as a leader in Israel. He immediately began to show his concern for the Jews under his control. In the space of a few days he organized a Social Welfare Department to set up soup kitchens for the hungry that served 500 meals daily and, in keeping with his interest in children, he made plans for schools to open with free lunches for all pupils. His energy animated others. He enlisted Left Poale Zion (Labor Zionist) functionaries, former principals of elementary schools, journalists, even the poet, Yitzchak Katzenelson, to help him in the worthy cause of furthering the education of Jewish children. Rumkowski saw to it also that the hospitals, homes for the aged, and other charitable institutions had food provided for them. The noninterference of the Germans with his work fostered illusions in him that he would be able to pursue the same policy of accommodation with the Germans that he had advocated with the anti-Semitic Polish regime.

The bubble soon burst. On the first of November, 1939, the Gestapo raided the Astoria coffee house, the chief gathering place for the intellectuals of Lodz, and arrested those present. Rumkowski promptly went to Gestapo headquarters to ask for their release. He was mocked, badly beaten, and thrown out bodily. On November 10, the four largest synagogues were burned to the ground. Worse was to follow. On the following morning, Rumkowski was ordered to call an emergency meeting of the Council of Elders. When all the elders had come together, uniformed, armed Germans entered the meeting hall, took away all personal documents, and arrested all but three. The three were Rumkowski himself, Samuel Faust, and David Windman, the latter two being freed on the pleadings of Rumkowski that they were his personal representatives. Of the others, twenty-four were shot after a period of imprisonment and torture, one died in prison, and the rest jailed to be later sent to Krakow. Of those, only two survived.

A new Council of Elders was ordered to be set up that same day. The news of the arrests had aroused such terror that Rumkowski had difficulty in recruiting communal activists. They felt that the unsought-for honor was only a preliminary to the grave. Special messengers were sent, however, to all the rabbis and to a sufficient number of other more or less prominent individuals to make an imposing audience for the Nazi colonel who addressed the gathering late that afternoon. Rumkowski was reconfirmed as "the Eldest of the Jews." All political parties were dissolved; administration was to be further systematized; Jewish cultural activities were permitted (Bar Mitzvahs, circumcisions, collections for Palestine, prayer meetings in private homes). Everyone was silent; the mildness of the orders on the heels of the morning's violence was incomprehensible. Rumkowski spoke up. He asked for the freedom of those arrested; the colonel said seven or eight would be released. A dispute arose over who was to be chosen, but Rumkowski refused to be a party to such a compromise. He wanted all to go free. The Nazi colonel made no concessions and kept no promises.

The raid on the Astoria coffee house and the arrests of the councilmen led to a mass exodus to the supposed safety of the General-Gouvernement. The very rich left, the school commission, intellectuals, and party functionaries so far untouched by the Germans. Unlike other communal leaders, so anxious to save their skins that they deserted their posts en masse, Rumkowski did not shirk his responsibilities. He made no attempt to flee. He felt to run away would be an admission of defeat on his part, a giving up of the great chance he had to distinguish himself in the eyes of his fellow-Jews, the only people who mattered to him. He was convinced that the barbarism of the Germans was only temporary, the result of their quick victory. He proceeded with his plans to launch the school system as the first step in the rebuilding of Jewish life in Lodz. A syllabus similar to that used before the war was adopted, arrangements made for a hot meal program for school children, even a special school for deaf-mutes planned for.

Sure now of his position, Rumkowski, had a rubber stamp made, "Mordecai Chaim Rumkowski, Eldest of the Jews of the City of Litzmannstadt." His next official act was to levy a heavy tax on merchants and factory owners for the support of the communal institutions. One of the merchants went to a former party comrade of Rumkowski's to have him intercede to lower the assessment. Rumkowski's reply was, "Sir, listen to me. If you were a stranger, I'd take you by the neck and throw you down the stairs, but since I know you practically as a kinsman, I'll tell you—don't mix in anything that doesn't concern you. The order is for real, not for a joke."

He meant what he said—when he ordered a thing done, it was to be done without question. He used his title and authority with the Germans as well as with the Jews. He asked the Germans for funds to support hospitals, old-age homes, and orphan asylums. He asked for repayment for the buildings confiscated by the Germans. He asked for unblocking of the frozen accounts in the local banks. Not all his requests were granted or even answered, but that made no difference to Rumkowski. He persisted, and perhaps by his very persistence he gained the confidence of the Germans as a forceful administrator.

He pushed too hard and too fast, however. On December 16, the members of the Council were called in, one by one, to be interviewed by a German official. Rumkowski sat silently by his side. They were informed that the Council's sole function was to execute the orders of the ruling power *and nothing else.* The Council, in order to increase its efficiency, was to be enlarged to a total of sixty-seven persons, with a presidium of ten, including a representative of the Gestapo.

Most of the new nominees, overwhelmed by this distinction, fled to Warsaw. Along with them went more intellectuals, industrialists, doctors, school executives, even the two men Rumkowski had saved from execution. Left to rebuild his advisory council from people previously inexperienced in communal affairs, Rumkowski did the best he could. He gladly took more responsibility on his own shoulders, applying his unquestioned organizational ability to the task of restoring a semblance of normal life to the Jewish community. No community can be said to be a community in the absence of elementary social functions such as the provision for food, medical care, shelter, and so on. The Germans had assigned a single function to the Council; Rumkowski recognized that more had to be done, and he proceeded to do it. At the same time he did not neglect the need to appease the Germans. With speed and diligence he carried out their command to register all the Jews, to him a harmless and meaningless statistical task.

4

The Germans originally planned to make of the whole of the Wartheland a purely German area by means of wholesale deportations of Poles and Jews to the General-Gouvernement, but conflicts arose in their own ranks. The General-Gouvernement did not want the deportees. While the arguments went on, many more Jews fled to the more congenial Polish atmosphere of Warsaw or to the safety of the Soviet-occupied areas.

On December 10, 1939, the *Regierungs-Präsident,* Ubelhoer,

realizing that he was not going to get rid of the Jews as fast as he had hoped, set up a secret commission to make preparations for the formation of a ghetto in Lodz. Secrecy was needed so that the movement of the Jews was to be sudden and precise, thus insuring that much Jewish property would be left behind and easily confiscated. Ubelhoer regarded the ghetto as a temporary institution. "I shall determine," he said, "at what time and with what means the Ghetto—and thereby the whole city—will be cleansed of Jews. In the end, at any rate, we must burn out this pestilence."

By February, 1940, all the plans were made. On the eighth of that month the orders were issued. All Jews were to move into part of the "Old City" and the sewerless Baluty slum district on the outskirts of the city, and all Poles and ethnic Germans were to move out of the area. With typical German efficiency, street by street in the city was emptied of Jews. Evasion and go-slow tactics were tried, but on March 6 and 7 about 200 Jews were shot on the streets and in their homes. After that prodding, the Jews wasted no time in going into the ghetto. There they were crowded together in the old houses, mostly wooden, without plumbing of any kind, with limited gas and electric supply. Ninety-five percent of the dwellings had no toilets, water, or sewer connections. By now the Jewish population of Lodz was only 164,000 (many had fled to eastern Poland, to the area occupied by the Soviet Union), but confining even that reduced number in such a small area raised many problems—for the Jews, not for the Germans.

Rumkowski met the problems head on. When non-Jews who owned relatively well-built houses refused to turn over the keys unless they were paid large sums of money, Rumkowski convinced the German authorities to intervene by arguing if a ghetto was to be for Jews, then all buildings in the ghetto should be made available without key-money being paid. Jews were limited in the amount of personal effects and clothing they could bring into the ghetto. Rumkowski persuaded the Germans to modify the order, with the result that in the guise of personal belongings large amounts of merchandise were brought in. When arguments arose among the newcomers about who was to live where and with whom, Rumkowski set up a Housing Office that assigned dwellings.

He also encouraged evasion of the German orders. Sometimes he argued with the German authorities when they demanded that he turn over to them machinery and raw materials left in various factories in the Baluty area, saying they could not be moved or could not be found. Sometimes he resisted passively by ignoring the communications sent to him. He was slowly testing the limits of German tolerance.

By May 1, all the Jews had been brought into the ghetto. (All, that is, except for about 100 rag-pickers and a handful regarded by the Germans as essential for organizing production in enterprises outside the ghetto. Later, in 1943, those exemptions were removed.) On May 10, the ghetto was closed. Police-President Schäfer ordered, "Jews must not leave the ghetto as a matter of principle. This order applies also to the Eldest of the Jews and to the chiefs of the Jewish police." The ghetto was encircled with barbed wire and guards posted at frequent intervals; later a board-and-picket fence was added. The first large ghetto in Europe since Jewish emancipation was established.

5

Rumkowski did not protest the establishment of the ghetto. Neither did the great mass of Shield-of-David-ornamented Jews nor those of their former leaders who remained. They believed that a ghetto would isolate them from pogroms, "wild actions," and unpredictable terroristic attacks. Rumkowski himself saw a positive aspect in the closed ghetto. It would be a miniature state, a Jewish state with a large degree of self-government. At the beginning of June, he said, "We have our own police, our own administration and post office, and we'll have our own currency."

Rumkowski's title developed new meaning. The German overlords preferred to deal with a single individual responsible to them rather than with a council. Rumkowski became the transmitter of German orders to the inhabitants of the ghetto. The Council of Elders lost even its advisory function because Rumkowski never called on it for advice. He was serene in his feeling that he knew best how to cope with the conquerors. He fancied himself as a modern version of the medieval Court Jew, a mediator between the rulers and the Chosen People, another Josef Süss Oppenheim.

He tried to undertake one of the functions of Court Jews—the rescue of his coreligionists from the hands of Amalek. During the earliest days of the ghetto, before the barbed wire was put up, some Jews had sneaked out to buy food in the city markets or to smuggle into the ghetto some of the belongings they had left behind. A number of them were caught by the Gestapo. Rumkowski gathered money from their families and from wealthy Jews so that he could ransom them from the Gestapo. Thinking the sum was insufficient, he appropriated from the Poor Fund of the former Kehillah enough to make up a total of 23,400 Reichsmarks. He offered the money as a ransom. It was taken from him and he was told to return the next day. At that time he was informed that the money was confiscated. The prisoners were not released. His effort to help, even though unsuccessful, was taken by the ghetto inhabitants as a sign he meant well. They also applauded his steadfastness in refusing to give to the Gestapo a list of wealthy Jews. In answer to those demands he said, "I have no children nor anyone in the world. I am ready to die."

Because they had no choice in the matter and because they too had illusions about history repeating itself in the form of medieval ghettos and Court Jews, the Jews began to cooperate with Rumkowski. They may not have liked the airs he put on, but they could see he was trying to help them. He was tireless in his efforts to make the transition to ghetto life easy, to make it mirror—distortedly, it is true, but that was not his fault—the past Jewish community. Adopting the bureaucratic methods of his masters, he gave orders right and left and saw to it that they were carried out. The thirty-eight schools were reduced to seventeen; the hospitals and other institutions were given suitable buildings. The unused Catholic Church of the Virgin Mary, in the ghetto, was guarded against provocatory acts. An extensive health system was built. Public relief and assistance were provided for the unemployed. For all these projects, administrative personnel was needed. In the absence of more experienced people, Rumkowski called on his old friends and acquaintances for help. The Housing Office, for example, was headed by Baruch Praszkier, a prewar Zionist leader. The ghetto police, "to maintain law and order," were under the command of Leon Rosenblatt, a bank clerk who had once been an officer in the Austrian army. Rumkowski was appreciative of their efforts. From then on, he had a soft spot in his heart for those who aided him in the early difficult days of organizing a functioning Jewish community. However, he never allowed such sentiment to deter him from dismissing any official who he thought was likely to contest his seat of power. Grumblings began to be heard in the ghetto, not against the German decrees but against the "dictator" Rumkowski. The crass vulgarity in the way he used the expression, "my Jews," offended the remaining political leaders of the underground parties. Rumkowski felt he needed their support. At first they rebuffed him, but he was not by any means a fool. Expressing a readiness to make concessions, he called a conference with the Bund, the Jewish Socialists. He allocated a quantity of sugar for its cooperatives; he refused, however, to permit it to set up its own children's kitchens—"the classic disunity of the Jews must be stopped at some point," he said. He asked the Bund for help in strengthening the Jewish police; the leadership turned down the request but could not keep many of the rank-and-file from joining the police force. He met with other parties as well, including the Communists. He offered them supplies for their cooperatives; he asked the Zionists to organize youth groups; he encouraged Poale Zion, Agudah Israel, and the Bund to enlarge their farm work in the outlying open areas of the ghetto, from which Polish peasants had been evacuated. All agreed he was a difficult and stubborn man to work with, but he might turn out to be a well-meaning and reasonable one in the long run. Rumkowski's answer to the Bund reflected his viewpoint of what the ghetto should be. He envisioned it as an autonomous (as far as the Germans permitted) national commune where justice and righteousness would prevail, where no Jew would suffer at the hands of another (except Rumkowski's in his role as a benevolent but stern father), where all would share equally until the time of terror would pass. Exploitation would not be allowed; commerce and industry would be regulated by the commune—with Rumkowski as the overlord. Health and education would be a communal responsibility—meaning Rumkowski's. His would be a model ghetto, a picture of the future New Jerusalem of the time of the coming of the Messiah. He felt that he was destined to be the savior of the Jews in this painful period of their history.

The facts of ghetto life were otherwise. True, no classes in the Marxian sense were present. The upper bourgeoisie were, for the most part, gone, their fortunes lost or their incomes cut off; the rich who remained lived by spending their capital or selling off their valuables. The petit bourgeoisie no longer existed. All were workers, and workers in a common cause—the survival of the Jewish people in their own persons. But nevertheless a kind of class society came to pass, although in Lodz, unlike what happened in Warsaw, the general poverty was so great that the spread between top and bottom was small. Around Rumkowski grew an ever-increasing circle of bureaucrats whose continued favored positions and special privileges depended on his goodwill. Jachimek, a Bundist, became the head of his Secretariat, to bring him petitions from "his people" and to recommend the appointment of officials. Emanuel Wolinsky, a Poale Zion (Labor Zionist) leader held another important post. These were exceptions, however. Most of Rumkowski's department heads were individuals previously inactive in Jewish communal life. A young lawyer, Henryk Naftalin, was his trusted adjutant, along with Zazhauer, a former merchant. On the principle of "set a thief to catch a thief," Rumkowski gave high posts in the police force to several underworld figures. The ghetto made jokes about the police force requirements: not six years of schooling but less than two years of imprisonment. The proletarian masses remained. Over them was the ghetto hierarchy, and over all reigned Rumkowski at the top of the social pyramid, "the Eldest of the Jews."

The ghetto laughed but made no objections when Rumkowski called his office "the Chancellery." All approved the system of "Block Elders" he organized to administer the "block fund," made up of more or less voluntary contributions from the wealthier inhabitants to make sure that no Jew went hungry. All applauded the Special Relief Bureau for the unemployed and for the familes of the workers sent to labor camps outside the ghetto. All agreed he was doing right by setting up a Control Commission to put down corruption in the various departments of his administration, even though Rumkowski's position was further enhanced by the Commission's activities. (The Control Commission was soon dissolved because of its inefficiency.) The working class groups, angered by the sale of the "better" dwellings to those Jews who had managed to bring part of their fortunes into the ghetto, were placated by Rumkowski's special taxes on the rich.

The most urgent problem in the ghetto was seeing that the people were fed. Food was sent in by the Germans but they demanded high prices for it; payment was made from the blocked accounts in the banks. The American Joint Distribution Committee sent to the Lodz Kehillah (which no longer existed) $20,000 which was converted by the Germans at the ridiculously low rate of five Reichsmarks to the dollar and then used by them as payment for the provisioning of the ghetto. The "Joint" also sent via Berlin 10,000 Reichsmarks for social welfare, to be distributed by the Bund. Rumkowski appropriated the entire amount, not for his own use but for the general welfare fund. A committee of the Bund protested that it should be allowed to set up its own apparatus to help its members (for whom the money was sent), but Rumkowski would not hear of that. "I alone handle the money here. I'll not permit any divided authority." To the *Kultussteuer* (religious community tax) permitted by the Germans, Rumkowski added a sliding tax on wages ranging from 1.5 percent to almost 10 percent. Ownership of real estate was not recognized; rent was paid into the ghetto treasury. With the exception of the tenement tax, Rumkowski paid no taxes into the general city treasury, on the grounds that no municipal services were provided to the ghetto.

Rumkowski, with 79 percent of the ghetto population on welfare, clearly saw that help from the outside world would be forthcoming neither regularly nor in sufficient amount. He felt no fear for the future. He had a positive program in mind—work! The ghetto had to be made self-supporting. Only one way was open for that—to start producing for the Germans. He had a series of conferences with Hans Biebow, the chief of the (German) Ghetto Administration. Biebow, a former merchant from Bremen with a degree in business administration, saw in a productive ghetto a chance to improve himself financially and to rise in the Nazi ranks. He encouraged Rumkowski in his design to set up factories in the ghetto; he got orders from the armaments industry for Rumkowski; he prevailed on higher officials to permit checks from abroad to be used as working capital to start ghetto industry; he even argued that the Jews should get more food so that they could produce more.

Slowly the wheels of industry began to turn in the ghetto. Textile manufactories, furniture shops, clothing and shoe factories, and a number of ancillary workshops began to function. The German idea of the "temporariness" of the ghetto fell into the background. The Germans could use the goods produced by the Jews. They cynically announced they would supply the raw materials and would pay for the finished products in food. "Let the Jews learn through suffering to be industrious workers, not parasites on Aryans." The Jews were doubly despoiled by the arrangement: raw materials were arbitrarily priced and the cost of the food supplied was calculated at a level 20 percent higher than that in the city.

Most of the factories were communal undertakings—"national," in Rumkowski's terminology—under the direction of the Eldest of the Jews and his deputies. A few producers' cooperatives were formed (leather workers, printers), and even fewer private firms began operating. The need for raw materials available only through the German Ghetto Administration via Rumkowski inevitably led to his taking over of the private enterprises. After the strikes of the winter of 1940-1941, the cooperatives were reorganized to become communal factories.

The economic advantage of a productive ghetto became increasingly patent to the Germans. Biebow, for example, hearing that the ghetto was scheduled to be a concentration point for 100,000 more Jews preliminary to their liquidation, strongly objected on the ground that the economic life of the ghetto would be disrupted and thus less money would be made for the Nazis (and him). Other officials agreed with him. Hefner, a Nazi leader from Posen, wrote to Adolf Eichmann in Berlin, ". . . I have the impression that Ubelhoer doesn't want the liquidation of the ghetto because he's making a good thing out of it. For example, there is the fact that in the special account for working Jews, each one brings in 6 Reichsmarks for an outlay of only 80 pfennigs." Greiser, the Gauleiter of the Wartheland, was well aware of the worth of the ghetto; he wanted his district *Judenrein,* but he also wanted the cash. He compromised with his principles: he said he would start by first getting rid of sick and unemployable Jews "for reasons of humanity" because those two groups were likely to spread infectious diseases.

Rumkowski knew why the Germans did not carry out their threat to remove the Jews from Lodz. He felt satisfaction that his policy was proving to be correct. To him, the problem of saving the Jews was a matter of simple common sense. Resistance being out of the question, all the Jews had to do was to prove that their work was necessary for the Reich and its army. They had to become so closely enmeshed in the fabric of the German war economy that it would be disrupted by dislocating the Jews. Talk of a *Judenrein* Wartheland would become utterly ridiculous once he had convinced the anti-Semites that coexistence was possible and that deportation was uncalled for. The thought of extermination never entered his mind.

In his role as Court Jew, Rumkowski used every means at his disposal to increase the provisioning of the ghetto, to circumvent the "legal" impoverishment of the Jews, and to improve living conditions. Sometimes he was successful, sometimes not. He took over the raw materials, machinery, and buildings held by German "trustees," and when they protested to higher authorities, he said he had no choice—they were too inefficient in their production of goods for the German army and he had to keep up his commitments, else both the Jews and the Wehrmacht would suffer in the long run. Flushed by his success, he asked Biebow for more doctors and more soap; at the bottom of his letter he wrote, "The preservation of health is my chief duty." Biebow did not bother to answer. Rumkowski was ordered to return certain goods left in the ghetto by Poles and ethnic Germans; he ignored the order and was supported by Biebow, who wanted no interference with his productive ghetto. Rumkowski asked for the return of the hospital equipment of the defunct Jewish hospitals outside the ghetto; he got it back for the minimal payment of 1,815 Reichsmarks. He wangled twenty-nine sewing machines (confiscated from Jews in the provincial hamlets) to help in the setting up of new factories. He repeatedly pressed the Germans to credit to the ghetto account the Polish and Czech debts paid off to Jewish industrialists since the closing of the ghetto.

He exerted every effort to see that the Jews were productively employed. He sent a letter to the German mayor reporting that he had 14,850 skilled workers available; he asked for orders for any or all of a list of seventy articles: clothing, shirts, corsets, knitwear of all types, pocketbooks, etc. He sent a similar letter two weeks later urgently asking for orders. He came to an agreement with the German administration whereby the latter gave 2,000,000 Reichsmarks as an advance on the value of goods pro-

Juced in order to set up a relief system, but he gave no relief without an understanding that anyone on public relief had to go to whatever work was assigned to him. He wrote to the German officials in various economic bureaus, pleading for more raw materials to be sent into the ghetto. He surreptitiously made contracts with private German firms until Biebow, anxious to preserve his arbitrary power over the ghetto, forbade such contracts. He encouraged inventiveness by giving awards (of extra food and privileges) to those who improved production or set up new factories. The latter were all communal institutions, their directors part of the ghetto bureaucracy, their products barterable through Biebow for food. Incentives for private enterprise were not given. "No Jew should take advantage of his starving brothers," said Rumkowski.

To insure that the meager food allotment was fairly distributed (and incidentally to eliminate profiteering in food and to control the soup kitchens of the clandestine political parties), Rumkowski instituted a system of food ration cards in June of 1940. From that time on, except for the insignificant black market, every ghetto inhabitant was dependent on the Provisioning Office for every type of food. The issuance of the ration cards became a weapon in Rumkowski's struggle with the workers.

He had to convince the ghetto population of the correctness of his "work" philosophy. As early as July, 1940, he said at a meeting of furniture workers, "Work is the essence of our existence . . . I have to prepare for a winter offensive of our own, for food and heating materials, and that's possible only if we work." His speech was greeted with laughter.

But the low rations soon changed the laughter into tears. Epidemics of typhus, typhoid, and dysentery caused the mortality rate in the ghetto to rise to staggering heights. The ghetto populace began to believe that Rumkowski's policy was the only one they could pursue. At least the factories provided the workers there with hot meals.

The workers followed Rumkowski but with dragging feet and sullen faces. The "socialization" of industry did not impress them.

Strikes and demonstrations broke out. The workers had many grievances: the pay was too low even to buy their quota of food on the ration cards, the hours of work were too long, the rationed food was too limited, the hot soup was too watery, favoritism and corruption existed in the rationing office. In August, 1940, a group know as the *shtarke* (the strong ones)—porters, butchers, draymen—demonstrated noisily and threatened Rumkowski's life. Rumkowski appeased them by selecting some of them as his personal bodyguard, thus assuring them the larger ration that was a perquisite of the ghetto bureaucracy. For others he made work and gave minor concessions. But he never forgave them for opposing him. When his power became stronger, at the first token of grumbling by the *shtarke,* he had them arrested and put on the list for work in the German labor camps, practically a death sentence. Textile workers and shoe workers struck, but Rumkowski appeased them too by trivial concessions and by allowing them to have shop stewards functioning in the factories. At the same time he tried to inflame the rest of the ghetto against the strikers. He issued a proclamation in the following words:

> Jews!
> What has happened recently is due to irresponsible elements who want to bring disorder into our lives. Those people have their own plans and they do not include constructive social help for the people.
> Stay quiet. Don't let yourselves be misled by irresponsible people who want to interfere with our present work and the plans for our future.

No documents exist that would indicate that the strikes and demonstrations were other than spontaneous or organized by leftist unions. Nevertheless, some of the slogans ("Kill Rumkowski!" "Open the Ghetto!") were so inflammatory that the Bund felt compelled to issue a statement saying that such slogans were the work of agents-provocateurs.

In September, 1940, Rumkowski, to answer the mounting complaints of the people, made an announcement: "In order to keep peace and quiet in the ghetto and to have no hungry people, I have instituted a new system of relief until I can get enough work for my factories and everyone will be able to get a job." He increased the relief allotments, he supplemented the wages of workers with families, he started new soup kitchens that served over 18,000 meals daily, he remitted the payment of rent. Those on welfare had to work where they were ordered to; those who refused such work were to be cut off the relief rolls. "I ask your goodwill and the fulfillment of your duties. I warn all who have the evil intent to violate law and order and who plan to obstruct my plans and who spread false rumors among the people—the punishment and repression I will bring on them will be even stronger and harsher than heretofore."

By October, Rumkowski was ready to teach the workers a lesson. He withdrew all the concessions and took away the right of the shop stewards to regulate hours and the rate of pay for work. He installed in each factory and workshop a commissar who was the whip to drive the workers to increasing productivity. Their weapon, besides actual physical force, was the ration card, which they could reduce as they wished for any infraction of labor discipline.

Rumkowski, obsessed with his work program, felt that any attempt to slow the pace of its development was a personal attack on him. He called a conference in December, 1940, of workers' delegates, administrative assistants, and factory executives. There, in response to criticism of his tactics by Moshe Lederman, a Bundist, and by another speaker, he stormed, "Strikers are criminals! I'll act like a dictator! I'll stamp them out, them and their families! I'll arrest them and send them to labor camps!" Rumkowski, the full power of the rationing system at his dispoasl, felt his might. He expressed it in tirades against those who drew relief and didn't work; he threw out threats of forced labor right and left. He meant what he said. He had murmurers dismissed from their jobs and added their names to the list of those scheduled for forced labor outside the ghetto.

The winter of 1940-1941 was bitter cold. The Germans prohibited the importation of coal or charcoal into the ghetto. What heating there was came from the limited supply of wood, augmented by that torn from dilapidated houses, even from garbage bins and privies. The frost and the near-starvation rations overcame the workers' fear of Rumkowski. On December 1, 1940, hospital workers went on strike and returned only after promises of better wages. Sporadic street demonstrations broke out, quickly put down by the Jewish police. At last, on January 23, 1941, the furniture workers started a sit-down strike for more rations. Rumkowski had the police drive the strikers from the factories. Resentment against the use of such force rose rapidly. In order to prevent a general strike, Rumkowski declared a lockout, closing all the factories. That meant one less meal a day for the workingman and a sharp reduction in rations for his family. In a few days, after a series of meetings with workers from various trades, he ordered special rations to be given to all but the furniture workers and had the factories reopened. The tailors went back to work, paying no heed to their being denounced as strike-breakers. ·Other trades followed. The furniture workers had to give in. The strike was broken. From that time on, Rumkowski reigned supreme over the workers. The shop stewards were discharged. The unions were dissolved. The workers' political parties were no longer recognized by Rumkowski as bodies to be reckoned with.

One evidence of his rigidly wielded authority was the temporary closing of all the tailoring factories on February 12, 1941. Rumkowski said the workers were practicing sabotage by their poor work, by their sending out uniforms without buttons, by making holes in the cloth, etc. He warned them that he would not tolerate such actions; he made an example of a couple of suspected ringleaders by arresting them. He reopened the workshops after that and noted with satisfaction how the quality of the work improved.

Authoritarian as he was, Rumkowski felt he had to make excuses for his actions and to justify his work program. But sometimes, in the course of his speeches, he got carried away, and then his vainglory appeared. For example, he said on one occasion after the strikes had been put down, "I assure you that I have no grudge against anyone. I put a few dozen people out of work, but that was actually being merciful to those agitators. Now what should I do? I have more important worries about upholding our existence. I declare openly—you're well off when you have a work assignment. . . . The leather cooperative workshop no longer exists. They're not the bosses over the shop. Quite the contrary. When I please I'll put in whom I will. The regulation of this painful question has cost me a lot of misery and ruined my health. But I didn't get scared by the agitators. I'm not getting mixed up with labor delegations or politicians . . ."

Work was the watchword. Rumkowski rigorously suppressed every opportunity for ventures that would free individuals from the organized ghetto economy. Smuggling of food and products, so vital for the circumvention of the Nazi starvation plan and to some extent successful in that direction in Warsaw, was harshly put down. Smuggling introduced an incalculable variable into the ghetto economy; smugglers, not dependent on Rumkowski for jobs or support, were a threat to his power. His police were efficient; smuggling decreased. Jewish and Polish smugglers suffered alike under the heavy hand of the police. For example, the police turned over to the Germans a Pole who had come through the barbed wire with a sack containing 4.75 kilograms of lard, 1.5 kilograms of butter, and four loaves of bread. Rumkowski's courts were equally efficient: smugglers were sent outside the ghetto to the German slave-labor camps, where few survived the inhumane treatment.

The ghetto currency was the most effective device in Rumkowski's hands; it put the final quietus to all smuggling. Rumkowski saw in the ghetto currency a protection against the activity of the German Criminal Police (Kripo). He took advantage of it as another arm of his despotism. He did not foresee what a potent force it would become against the survival of "his Jews."

Rumkowski could not maintain law and order in the ghetto unless the lawlessness of the Germans was curbed. The Kripo, one of whose functions was to confiscate hidden Jewish valuables, was the worst offender of all in their capricious searches and seizures, always accompanied by violence and bloodshed. To forestall the Kripo and to "eliminate the sale of personal goods for low prices," Rumkowski opened a Purchasing Office for the acquisition of foreign currency, jewels, crystal-ware, and porcelain. Their value was assessed by experts; the owners were recompensed in receipts for Reichsmarks; the articles so purchased were turned over to the Germans in exchange for food. Workers were also paid in such receipts, which soon became the most convenient medium of exchange within the ghetto. The receipts were known as "Rumkes"; they were beautiful banknotes ornamented with the Shield of David, Rumkowski's portrait, and emblems of ghetto industry. When Rumkowski was asked what backing the currency had, he replied, "It is backed by my work and the work of the ghetto."

The ghetto currency was very effective in stopping smuggling; worthless outside the ghetto, it could not be used to pay for food brought in. Rumkowski ordered that after May 28, 1940, Reichsmarks could not be used to pay for anything; only the Rumkes, technically receipts for Reichsmarks, had any exchange value. The ghetto people hastened to turn in their Reichsmarks, their foreign currency, their gold and silver coins; in a short time, 7,348,000 Reichsmarks were deposited to the ghetto accounts. For his ingenuity in thus squeezing out of the Jews their hidden capital, the Germans praised Rumkowski highly. The same praise was forthcoming as the *objects d'art*, the gold watches, the diamonds and other jewelry were turned over to the German administration.

Rumkowski prided himself on the establishment of his Purchasing Office and the ghetto currency. He said, "Too many people are disposing of their valuables at ridiculously low prices on the black market. I'm helping them get a fair price for their goods." He saw with satisfaction the cessation of smuggling and the decreased activity of the Kripo. He did not see that his "bank," the issuer of the ghetto currency, was not, as he imagined, the peak of ghetto autonomy, the very symbol of independence, but rather an invisible rope around the ghetto, a rope that cut it off effectively from the rest of the world.

Notwithstanding his measures against the factory workers, Rumkowski never forgot that as a Court Jew he had to alleviate the distress of "his Jews." The amount of food allotted to the ghetto was proportionate to its population; the Germans ordered a census. Rumkowski dilly-dallied on one pretext or another until he was frightened by threats of dire punishment. He then gave the figure as 160,000, undoubtedly exaggerated. The Germans asked for a complete list of those who got food parcels from abroad so that an equivalent amount could be deducted from the ghetto provisioning; Rumkowski promised a prompt reply and as promptly "forgot" his promise. Biebow commanded that the factories make special hats for the ghetto officials; Rumkowski turned aside the command because such production was uneconomical for the ghetto, since the hats could not be traded for food.

Rumkowski used the labor unrest as an argument in dealing with the Germans. He convinced them, especially Biebow, who got a rake-off from all ghetto industry, that it was to their advantage that all ghetto workers be fully employed, that the rate of profit was high, that Jewish productivity surpassed that of Poles. New contracts were given; more raw materials were sent in; unemployment diminished rapidly; official "Help Wanted" advertisements appeared in the *Ghetto-Zeitung*. And as spring came, the Jews again looked on Rumkowski as doing the best he could for them. They chuckled when he put on the stupid act for Biebow, telling him he found it impossible to locate those Jews who owed money to Poles and Germans in Lodz. They laughed when Rumkowski, directed to turn over immediately all non-Jewish possessions left behind in the ghetto, said he didn't know the addresses, didn't have the keys, had no staff to take inventory, and had no trucks with which to move materials. They nodded their heads in satisfaction when they saw new roadways being built, a new railroad station, and a new trolley car line for the ghetto. With all his faults, Rumkowski was prevailing over the Germans, they felt. Ghetto life was awful, but "one can survive."

Rumkowski's endeavors to stabilize ghetto life took on various forms, all under the supervision of trusted henchmen and all intended to show "his Jews" what a benevolent despot he was. He pleased the pious by proclaiming Saturday as the official day of rest. He increased relief payments "in spite of the severe financial situation." He expanded the health services. He organized work programs for the unemployed and made sure that the orphan asylums and homes for the aged had adequate provisioning. And with every enlargement of communal activities, the number of bureaucrats increased. In the five months from February to July, 1941, the figure of direct employees in the ghetto administration rose from 550 to 7,316. Employment as a ghetto official carried with it more food, a great desideratum. Later, in 1942, a more important fringe benefit was added in the form of life itself.

Rumkowski's power grew, largely because of the ready weapon he had against any opponent—the ration card, removal of which was equivalent to a death sentence from starvation. He closed the organizational soup kitchens and substituted communal ones in order to weaken the underground political parties. He eliminated the Bundist and Zionist agricultural *kibbutzim* in the Marysin section and put the orchards and farms under the general ghetto administration. He set up a Summary Court for the quick sentencing of offenders against his orders. He ordered house searches for the detection of thefts from the communal factories, saying, "Who steals from the ghetto steals from all Israel." Offenders were usually punished not by imprisonment but by working nine hours a day in ghetto communal institutions; they received less than the regular wage. More brazen offenders (those who were late to work or who refused to obey the factory overseers) were jailed. Sentences were severe: Shlomo Hendel, aged thirty, was given six months at hard labor for stealing a pair of trousers from the factory where he worked; Aba Reiber, twenty-one, one month imprisonment for stealing a piece of wood; Jacob Frenkel, thirty, one month hard labor for remaining on relief when a job was open for him in a factory; Abraham Gottlieb, two months for stealing two loaves of bread; Joseph Sarna, thirty-eight, three weeks hard labor for stealing potatoes, and his wife, Hodel, a month for inciting him to steal. Twenty-four Poale Zionists were imprisoned for holding a private meeting, prima-facie proof to Rumkowski of subversive activity against "the Eldest of the Jews." In response to a delegation of rabbis who had paraded with the Scrolls of the Law asking for more food for the people, Rumkowski called a conference of all the rabbis, condemned the "sacrilege," took away the ration cards of the demonstrators—and coopted some into his administration. *Divide et impera.*

His own police force was not exempt from his anger. In February, 1941, he discharged a number of policemen for brutality and others for taking bribes. "Why do I need so many policemen if they're crooks?" he asked rhetorically. "It's better for them to work. I can get honest policemen."

Corruption and graft were widespread in the ghetto. Rumkowski fulminated against the swindlers and confidence men who preyed on the masses, such as the fakers who collected money for nonexistent parcels to be delivered from the post office. He would hear no complaints, however, against those of his favorites who were accused of misappropriating food. An attack on his courtiers was an attack on him.

Rumkowski did not view himself as an iron-fisted overlord but rather as a benevolent patriarch whose chastisements of "his Jews" were as painful to him as the recipients thereof. If one hand was heavy, the other was light and beneficent. Before the Jewish New Year in 1941 he sent every child between the ages of two and seven packages of candy and coupons for two extra meals for the holiday. The candy was wrapped with a paper reading, "In honor of the New Year, from your President, Chaim Rumkowski."

The food question was paramount in the ghetto. A sample ration for June, 1941, contained 2.25 kilograms of bread for workers, 1.14 kilos for the unemployed; horse meat for workers, 200 grams a week, for the unemployed, 160 grams, but since there was no meat for the latter, two eggs were substituted; fats, 100 grams a week; potatoes, 5.25 kilos a month; sugar, 600 grams a month. Actually these were paper rations; the norm was never reached.

Rumkowski, in his role as intercessor for the Jews, argued constantly with the Germans about the quantity and quality of the provisions sold to the ghetto. He never quibbled about the price he had to pay, so anxious was he just to get the food. But he politely refused on more than one occasion to buy "great bargains" in spoiled canned goods. Sometimes the Germans outwitted him; for example, once he was sent 1,517 kilos of meat, but only 800 kilos were usable, 200 kilos were going bad and had to be cooked immediately, and the rest had to be thrown out—but paid for. Rumkowski prevailed on Biebow to protest to Berlin that the malnutrition among the Jews was impairing their efficiency in production. He lied to the Germans about the number of employed and about the health situation in order to get more food sent in. He persuaded the Germans to provide extra flour so that matzoth for Passover could be baked to be sold at cost.

Nevertheless, hunger and malnutrition spread, leading to such debility that death occurred when the slightest infection supervened. (The Germans forbade the naming of starvation as the cause of death in statistical reports.) Murmurings began to be heard. "If Rumkowski's as great as he says he is," people asked, "why don't we get more food?" A litterateur put out privately a few issues of a journal, in one of which the poem, "The Ration," appeared:

We have to go to Rumkowski's house,
"We're hungry," we have to yell.
We won't shut up for him,
We can't shut up for him.
Knock out all his windows!
The ration cards have little worth,
Here we live in hell on earth.

＊   ＊   ＊

No matter how he tried, providing enough food was not in Rumkowski's power. He tried to make up for the deficiency in food by "normalizing" ghetto life. In place of the schools ordered closed by the Germans, Rumkowski established a new school system, with instruction in Yiddish, Hebrew, Bible, and Jewish history. The official language was to be Yiddish, but unfortunately most of the teachers had been so assimilated into Polish culture that they knew no Yiddish, and therefore the opening of the schools had to be delayed until the teachers completed special crash seminars in which they learned their "mother tongue." Then Rumkowski had placards put up:

Dear children!
You know how much I love you. Even in the days of my orphan asylum I constantly thought of and worried about you. Today I no longer have the possibility of helping you as I would like to, but better times will come. . . . Meanwhile, dear children, go to school. Let the school be a warm home to you. Study and grow up to be decent human beings. Don't loiter on the streets. Stay away from the [ghetto] walls. . . . As much as possible I want to be a father to you.

The Eldest of the Jews
Ch. Rumkowski

Rumkowski was sincere when he said he was concerned about the children. He did more than was expected of him. A school health service was instituted; a division of this service got extra food to combat childhood tuberculosis. In the outlying Marysin district of the ghetto, day camps, new orphan asylums, and technical schools were set up, each with its own medical team to insure that the children were well taken care of.

The general medical services were further reorganized and expanded. Theaters were opened; concerts and lectures were given. Defeatist themes were taboo. The "Ghetto Lullaby," changed from the traditional "Raisins and Almonds," to "Close your eyes, my little one. Here there are no almonds, no raisins for you, only bitter, bitter days . . ." was forbidden to be sung; it was too sad a reminder of the distorted Jewish life of Litzmannstadt.

Rumkowski drove around the ghetto in a horse and carriage exuding goodwill, seizing every occasion to make a speech to "his Jews" in which he promised them that through his efforts they would survive the war.

Rumkowski, who before the war had had to fight for recognition from his fellow-Jews, now reveled in the respect given to him, a respect that arose from his dictatorial powers. The synagogues prayed for his continued health and well-being as they had prayed for the Tsar, the Kaiser, and all their former rulers. Never a modest man, Rumkowski encouraged flattery and sycophancy. Word of mouth was not enough for him to spread the tidings of his goodness. He ordered the publication of the *Ghetto-Zeitung*, a newspaper in which he was lauded to the skies as a True Judge, a *Lamed-Vovnik* (one of God's fabled Thirty-six Just Men), the Savior of the Jews of Litzmannstadt. The people read: "The Eldest says. . . . The President orders. . . . The Chairman commands. . . ." His praiseworthy aims for the ghetto were stated as: "Work, Bread, Care for the Sick, Protection of the Children, and Law and Order." Rumkowski said of these aims, "From this program I'll not budge an inch," and "As long as my heart beats, I'll stand guardian over your interests." Poems of praise were regular features of the paper. A typical panegyric:

Our President, Herr Rumkowski,
Besides his brains and talents
Is blessed by Heaven
With a firm, strong hand . . .
    In the factories, in the offices,
    All base elements are now put away.
    Order reigns in the ghetto
    Thanks to his firm, strong hand.

* * *

His incredibly vainglorious speeches were quoted in adulatory detail: "I am smarter than anyone else and the Jews in the ghetto have only one person they should follow—me. . . . My eyes are always open and my head thinks clearly about every detail in the ghetto. . . ." He was not ashamed to receive as a gift a miniature silver cover for the Book of Esther on which was inscribed: "In lasting remembrance of his exalted eminence, etc. . . ."

So certain was Rumkowski that he would be known as an important figure in Jewish history that he wanted to make sure no detail of his rule would be overlooked by historians in the future. He steadily enlarged the Archival Bureau, coopting for it journalists, writers, and poets, all of whom had the task of recording his words and deeds for posterity. Paintings and posters abounded showing Rumkowski standing guard over the sleeping ghetto or spreading his mantle around the hungry and the children. Parades were held in his honor and complimentary albums presented to him. His vanity knew no bounds; the oath taken in the courts was "before God, man, and the Eldest of the Jews."

Rumkowski used the *Ghetto-Zeitung* as an official organ for his announcements and pronouncements. In the very first issue he wrote (at least the editorial appeared over his name), "The *Ghetto-Zeitung* will not permit all kinds of troublemakers and agitators with evil intentions to spread irresponsible rumors that only serve to bring about disquiet and chaos among the people." His threats were published verbatim: "Arrest or money fine or both for the unemployed who refuse to follow the orders of the House Administrators to clean up the litter in the streets and courtyards." His slogans were displayed as headlines: "In the ghetto there should be no clock-watching at work." Over the reports of "criminals" punished by the Summary Courts he had put "Read and Take to Heart!"

On December 27, 1941, Rumkowski married Dora Weinberger, a thirty-year-old lawyer who had been accredited to the Lodz Municipal Court. Rabbi Feiner presided over the services. Present were the entire rabbinate and the heads of all the ghetto departments. The reception that followed the nuptials was sumptuous in the eyes of the hungry ghetto populace. The favored guests were served with fish, roast meat, compôte, six pies, other sweets, brandy, wine, and liqueurs. Congratulatory messages poured in from all sides; the senders hoped for additional rations in exchange for their good wishes. During the festivities a few coarse May-December jokes were cracked at Rumkowski's expense. He got angry, lost his temper, and threatened the jokesters with transportation to labor camps.

His feelings were also hurt when the Germans forbade the use of the postage stamps he had printed bearing his likeness and the Shield of David.

They stepped on his toes in another field as well. They cared little about his vanities but they would brook no interference with their provisioning of the ghetto. The successful growing of vegetables in the Marysin area that Rumkowski had counted on as a backlog against the uncertain food deliveries of the Germans gave the latter an excuse to reduce the amount of food sent in. Rumkowski was constrained to barter the produce for staple food items.

6

His "planned economy" was further disturbed by the influx of Jews deported from provincial hamlets. Most of the deportees were men broken in spirit; their wives and children had been sent "elsewhere." Places had to be found for the newcomers in the workshops in order to get them off the relief rolls. Rumkowski resented them as intruders and carriers of unbelievable atrocity stories.

Then came the 20,000 Jews sent into the ghetto from Prague, Luxemburg, Vienna, Berlin and other German cities. The German mayor of Litzmannstadt on behalf of the German Ghetto Administration had made a sharp protest against their entry. He said the ghetto was already crowded and those who dwelt there had "incredibly poor living conditions. There would simply be no room, even if the newcomers were placed in barracks. Neither work nor food would be available for the Western Jews [plus the

5,000 Gypsies expected] because 80 percent of the cost of the provisioning of the ghetto was borne by the goods produced and no
new orders were coming in." But higher German authorites were
not interested, as the local Germans were, in making a profit by
squeezing labor out of the Jews. They were interested only in wiping them out. The Gypsies (4,989 in all, 11 having died en route)
and 19,837 Jews came into the ghetto.

The Western European Jews were a grievous thorn in Rumkowski's side. He needed artisans and workers for his productive
ghetto; most of the newcomers were old men and women,
businessmen, lawyers, physicians, and other professionals. On the
one hand he respected their greater "culture"; on the other, he
knew of their traditional denigration of the Polish Jews, and he
worried about the possibility that they might criticize his administration to their "Aryan" compatriots. He feared that they would
try to supplant him or bypass his authority by dealing directly
with the Germans. His worry was needless; the German Jews, well
conditioned to obedience, were as subservient to his rule as were
the native *Ostjuden.*

Regardless of their attitude, the Western European Jews
created new problems for the ghetto. The SS took a special interest in the German Jews: the sick and weak were placed in barracks
and given extra care; the rest were housed in the school buildings,
there being no other places available. That was the end of the
educational system of which Rumkowski was so proud. Still there
was overcrowding—quickly remedied by the Germans. They shot
the patients in the insane asylum and in the home for incurables
because "the Reich would not support nonproductive Jews" and
the latter took up room needed for the Western European Jews.
The brutality with which this action took place sent a chill of horror through the ghetto; all feared that the early period of violence
was to be repeated. No further terroristic acts took place, however, and the ghetto population accepted the explanation the Germans gave them. The cultural groups, the choruses, theaters, and
the symphony orchestra eagerly absorbed the new talent the Germans had forced on them.

Worse for Rumkowski's plan for a stabilized productive ghetto than the qualitative and quantitative population change was the inflation that followed the advent of the Western European Jews. They had brought with them many valuables which they did not sell through the Purchasing Office, preferring to barter them for food on the black market. Rumkowski thundered and cursed at the "foreigners" who were disrupting the economy of the ghetto and who by their mere presence were causing juvenile delinquency. The schools being closed, children wandered the streets, stealing what food they could or digging in the garbage heaps for a stray lump of coal or a moldy, leftover potato. Rumkowski said he would put a stop to the children's criminality. He set up a special Juvenile Court to which was attached a reformatory—characteristically for the "work ghetto", in the form of a workshop.

Inflation was further accelerated by the pensions remitted by the German government to war veterans and retired dignitaries. Rumkowski met that problem head on. In charge of the distribution of these monies, he exchanged the Reichsmarks for Rumkes but, fearful of possible complaints from the German Jews to the state offices, he used two thirds of the sum for their needs. Food parcels sent in to the Western Jews were confiscated for use in the hospitals. Such was the corruption in his administration that many of the parcels found their way to the black market.

More people in the ghetto meant that more food was needed—and thus greater productivity. Originally Rumkowski had expressed his care for the aged by setting up homes for them and by giving them special rations. Now they became a burden to him. He announced that everyone physically able to work would have to do so. Old men and women became sorters of goods, splitters of mica crystals, winders of coils. Rumkowski's speeches became more frantic. In one speech at the time he said, "Forty thousand men are now working in the factories. The budget will be increased to include 10,000 more . . ." And after describing his efforts to better conditions, he concluded with appeals to keep order and with threats of dire punishment. "Help me uproot the forbidden radio apparatus, if any exists in the ghetto. Don't politic. Just work and work. Otherwise blood will run." And in answer to why he called no meetings of the Advisory Council, he justified himself by saying, "I don't need a *Beirat* to obstruct my work. I take from the rich to give to the poor."

Rumkowski acted boldly, but he was ever conscious of his limited education vis-à-vis the German Jews. To cover up, he blustered and threatened. "Don't think you're so smart," he said to the German Jews. "Knock out of your heads the idea that you'll become leaders in the ghetto." In a later speech he said, "It's not enough I have to deal with my own wise guys—now I have new ones from the Reich. They think they're the best in the world and they want to be the bosses. They're making a big mistake. Take care! One interference with my orders and they'll feel the full weight of my hand." At a later meeting when Western European Jews complained about their living conditions, he ranted, "You want to run things like you used to. You think you're the smartest and the best, the cream of the crop. You're dead wrong. I tell you—watch your step. Once you disobey my orders, I'll have to quiet you down. I won't be held back from the sharpest measures. For that I have the power and the strength."

The cultural and religious activities that flourished in this period were a curious mélange of hankering after the "old days" and a wish to survive the new, if only by pretending that normal life was possible. Rumkowski watched jealously over every phase of cultural life lest his authority be lessened. The only party kitchen still permitted was the "intelligentsia kitchen" run by Helena Rumkowski, his sister-in-law, under the egis of the General Zionists. The Bundists and Zionists used choruses and drama groups as a mask for their forbidden political activities. The secret Communist cells carried on studies of Marx's works. Rumkowski knew what was going on, but he winked at it because he felt the ghetto workers needed amusements to keep their minds off their troubles. Only when the groups became bolder and began to assert their independence of the ghetto authorities did Rumkowski step in and substitute for them a House of Culture, an official ghetto enterprise and another source of patronage. He also encouraged the formation of sports clubs (mainly soccer teams) and became their patron. He was inconsistent about higher education: first he allowed college-level courses to be taught privately, then he forbade them, then allowed them again.

His folk attitude toward religion dominated the entire religious atmosphere. He permitted a *minyan* (religious quorum) if it was requested of him, despite the new German ban on private religious gatherings. On the High Holy Days he attended a synagogue that he opened in a former movie house. As long as possible he maintained Saturday as the day of rest, switching to Sunday only after repeated orders by the Germans. He gave special ration cards for Passover to the very orthodox (and to his special favorites). He supported the rabbis by a monthly stipend but did not allow them to receive honoraria; any fees they collected were to be turned over to the common fund of the ghetto. He authorized the rabbis to hold rabbinical courts for the settlement of disputes except when the disputes concerned money. The Rabbinical Council was completely subservient to him; at his request they decided pregnant women and those Jews who felt weak or ill from lack of food could eat horse meat, the only kind of meat available; they ended their communications to him with the phrase, "with the greatest respect." Rumkowski enjoyed being the center of attention. Late in 1942 (after most of the rabbis had been deported) he took over one of the functions of the rabbinate by performing weddings himself; he changed the form of the service by omitting the charge on the groom to support his wife; his gift to the newlyweds was a half kilogram of honey and two extra rations of bread. Under pressure from the Germans he thundered against some observances of ancient customs; he ordered beards and side-curls to be shorn and the long gabardines of pious Jews to be cast aside. He empowered the Jewish police to shave forcibly all except duly ordained rabbis and aged men they found with beards and earlocks, never considering that that was exactly what the Nazis had done in the early days of their hooliganism. He was tolerant, however, of the religious brotherhoods that sprang up for placing mezuzahs (doorpost charms) on houses, for observance of the laws for washing the hands and saying grace before food, and for visiting the sick; he opposed, naturally, the Society of the Guardians of the Sabbath as interfering with factory production.

He turned his back in anger on the German-Jewish converts, both Catholic and Protestant, who requested prayer meeting houses and religious instruction for their children. "In the ghetto," he said, "you have nothing to do with religion. Everyone who wears the yellow patch is a Jew. If you're not satisfied with my answer, go write to the Gestapo to let you out. I'll gladly let you go. Meanwhile, while you're with us, you're Jews. Don't fool yourselves that I'll do more for you than for other Jews. You don't want to mix with us? Then go away. I won't have any regrets."

His reply to the Christian Jews was widely quoted and approved of by the "old inhabitants" of the ghetto. They also approved, as evidence of his personal integrity, his dismissal of the officials of the Control Office, a hotbed of favoritism and corruption. A diarist wrote, "Maybe the President is right when he complains that he is surrounded by thieves."

Some of the Western Jews were assimilated. New workshops sprang up—and tuberculosis, even before the war a plague in Lodz, increased. More than 85 percent of the population worked in industry, earning over 16,000,000 Reichsmarks. And more than 60 percent had active tuberculosis. Productivity rose to new heights—and the "ghettocracy," as the ghetto administration was called, comprised about 13,000 individuals, almost all of them toadying and fawning on Rumkowski. The *Ghetto-Zeitung* described Rumkowski's headquarters thus:

> A whole staff works there, and over all and everything is the ever-watchful eye and the active mind of President Rumkowski . . . The President sits in his private office from early morning and studies carefully every document . . . He knows what goes on in every corner of his factories, workshops, offices, etc. . . .

He may have known about everything, but some things he preferred to ignore. Along with the rise of administrative personnel went graft and favoritism. Those in charge of food distribution put aside extra portions for themselves, their families, and their friends. Rumkowski threatened the "thieves, swindlers, and criminals who work in my offices," but he needed their support. Except in rare instances the threats were not carried out but when they were, the judgment was terrible. Such was Rumkowski's rage at what he regarded as disloyalty to himself that the dismissed functionaries were refused work permits even as common laborers, a ruling equivalent to a death sentence. Nevertheless, corruption, embezzlement, and "protection" increased. The police force had its own rackets: bribes were taken to release men from jail, for overlooking violations of the sanitary ordinances, for winking at the private sale of goods. Nothing was too petty for police graft. A ghetto song described how the police regulated the queues for horse meat: for a tip one could go to the head of the line, so that eventually all that was left for the others was bones.

The ghetto was visited frequently by various German commissions. They had nothing but praise for its operations and recommended that delegations from other ghettos be sent to see how a ghetto should really operate. The Germans expressed satisfaction at the good work the Jews were doing for the Wehrmacht. Only one commission had a criticism: the courts were too lenient —that is, the Jewish judges did not impose death sentences for "crimes" such as listening to Allied radio broadcasts. Rumkowski, eager to show the Germans he was fully cooperative, commanded the judges to do as the Germans wished. The judges resigned en masse rather than sentence their fellow-Jews to death. Rumkowski took away their ration cards, but a secret committee of intellectuals collected money for them and supported them. A compromise was finally reached. A few judges returned to their posts, and the question of capital punishment was quietly dropped. The other ex-judges bore the full brunt of Rumkowski's displeasure. They were ordered to report for jobs at hard labor and were among the first to be included in the coming death transports.

The praise he received from the Germans convinced Rumkowski that his "work policy" was proving correct. He also hailed, despite the inconveniences they caused him, the importations of the Jews from the hamlets and from Western Europe as an omen that his ghetto was to be permanent, not temporary, as in other parts of Nazi-occupied Poland. The ghetto Jews felt as he did. To them it was inconceivable that the Germans would use transportation so desperately needed for the war effort merely to shuttle Jews back and forth.

The Jews shut their eyes to the fate of the Gypsies. Rumkowski was ordered to set up special barracks for them, to provide food and medical services, and to see that the dead were buried in the Jewish cemetery. A typhus epidemic, in which several Jewish doctors lost their lives, broke out in the Gypsies' quarters. They were strictly quarantined during their short-lived existence in the ghetto. In December, 1941, they were deported. The Jews neither knew where nor cared. The Gypsies ended at the death camp of Chelmno.

The Ghetto of Litzmannstadt was isolated from ghettos elsewhere, so well sealed off that the Jews in Warsaw, with no further news from Lodz, concluded that it had been liquidated. In Vilna, however, it was believed that the ghetto still remained, unique among all other ghettos in that in Lodz there was relative safety, with neither mass executions nor fake resettlements.

Indeed, the Ghetto of Lodz was quiet. It was self-contained, with little interference from the Germans. They had no need to interfere; Rumkowski was their efficient agent. No Germans appeared in the ghetto to use Jews for target practice, as in Warsaw; the only shootings that took place were when a Jew came too close to the ghetto boundaries. Malnutrition and starvation were present but not to the extent as in Warsaw, and no naked dead bodies lay around in the streets. Law and order was the rule—Rumkowski's law and order. He prided himself on his "productive ghetto." Life was not pleasant there for "his Jews," but at least they had life in familiar surroundings.

7

In the same month that the Gypsies were removed to their unknown destination, while Rumkowski was congratulating himself on the success of his "work policy", came the orders from the Germans to select 20,000 Jews for "resettlement elsewhere," the deportations to start in January of 1942. The Germans left the selections up to Rumkowski. They had no doubt that he would carry out these orders as faithfully as he had carried out others. Rumkowski did not like the idea of losing so many of "his Jews." He pleaded with the authorities and got a promise to have the number reduced to 10,000. The Germans said that the deportations were necessary to get rid of unemployables, a plausible reason to Rumkowski, fitting in with his work policy. He persuaded himself that the deportations were fresh proof that the ghetto was to be a permanent work-place for Jews, unlike the already liquidated smaller ghettos of the province. He did not know (nor did anyone else in the ghetto) of the death camp at Chelmno. He regretted the coming deportations because he felt (and was told by the Germans) that the Jews would be going to labor camps or to work on farms under primitive conditions where they would have to undergo such hardships that they would surely die there. That he expected such an end for them is seen in his speech of January 25, 1942, toward the final stages of the first deportation, when he said, "The Jews in the ghetto criticize me because I didn't foresee the catastrophe. Deportation alone isn't the worst. . . . In open I can't say more."

When he announced the decree, Rumkowski tried to forestall murmurings by taking the offensive. He scolded his hearers. "The ghetto is autonomous. . . . The Eldest of the Jews alone can decide who is to be sent out. . . . I have it on high authority they will be resettled somewhere in the provinces. . . . This decree is the result of the loafers, the reliefers who won't work, the politicians, the newcomers who have changed the character of our formerly safe ghetto. . . . Dark clouds hang over us Jews here in Litzmannstadt. I won't take all the responsibility on myself. I have in you living witnesses that I've warned you before now. If I weren't ashamed, I'd cry like a baby and beg of you to help me out of my troubles. . . ." And then, ever the lord and master, he continued, "Whoever opposes me will be arrested. . . . This action will be carried out. . . ." He said he would pick first the criminals, then the speculators, then those on relief, and those who refused to work where they were assigned.

The threats concealed his fear of taking the onus for the selections. Now he sought advice. Some of his advisers said to send out the old and the sick to ease the burden on the ghetto; others said the young and strong should be sent out because the Germans were not to be trusted and the deportees were probably going to be sent far away (death was not even thought of) and the young could survive the rigors of the journey; still others said that whole families should go so that the strong could help the weak. The Rabbinical Council refused to give any opinion: "it was not their responsibility." The political parties declined cooperation in making the selections, not to their credit, however; they had plans of their own to save their comrades. Rumkowski finally evolved a "humane" plan: the deported were to consist of (1) 2,000 refugees from the provincial towns—they would be happier in more familiar surroundings, (2) the families of those men sent outside the ghetto for slave labor—they would have a better chance of being reunited with their menfolk, (3) the families on relief—their going would enable productive workers to get more food, (4) the "criminals"—those whose names appeared on the Central Card Index as having been arrested for any reason whatsoever, from knocking over a garbage can to stealing a piece of wood for fuel, and (5) of course, anyone who had ever been an "enemy"—of Rumkowski's.

Such was the demoralization in the ghetto, not all of which was Rumkowski's fault, that no organized protest or resistance arose. Pleas for mercy came only from individuals, and those pleas indicate the fears and the tragic conditions under which the Jews of Litzmannstadt lived. A sampling of the letters to the Deportations Committee:

Abraham Leib Fischof: "I received notice that I am to be sent out, probably because my son, Isaac Moshe, twenty years old, when he worked in Marysin took a piece of wood to make a fire and he was sentenced to three months imprisonment for that. He served his sentence and then was sent out of the ghetto. The guilty person is no longer here, and I plead with you not to punish me because of an error committed by a young lad."

Deborah Einesman: asked not to be sent out because she is nursing a ten-month-old baby. "I presume I am being evacuated because my husband was sent to a labor camp in Germany, but I want to point out that I never had a good life with him and separated from him."

Jacob Gershon Berkovitch: "Send me and my wife out, not our eighteen-month-old child."

Samuel Hersh Eilenberg: asked not to send out his family of seven persons. "I and my two sisters, Gittel and Shulamith, are working. My sixty-four-year-old father is not working because he is sick. If the request to save all is denied, then send out my father and let the others go." Attached to the letter was a certificate from a tailor factory that Eilenberg was an industrious and steady worker.

Abraham Barkovski: complains that his family shouldn't go because he didn't fall in any of the categories; the only reason he can find is that the family lives in the same house as Moshe Banker, who was sent out of the ghetto previously; the family didn't choose to live with Banker but were given the dwelling by the ghetto authorities.

Wolf Eige: "If the expulsion order is related to the sentence my son received, I have the honor to explain: my son died seven weeks ago. Therefore I believe that at the moment of is death me and my family's responsibility for his error was wiped out . . . I work hard as a porter and am satisfied with my work."

Evasion was impossible. Corrupt as Rumkowski's bureaucracy was, when it came to keeping lists of names and addresses it was efficient. The house administrators were ordered, under penalty of their own deportation, to report any strangers in their houses; the inhabitants were threatened with the same fate for feeding or keeping anyone overnight. No rations were given out, and work in the factories was suspended. The sale or barter of food was forbidden. The selections and filling of transports went like clockwork. Everyone cooperated and everyone tried to take advantage of the situation. Bribes were accepted for the removal of names from the list of those scheduled for deportation. The political parties had their clerk-members who worked in the ghetto offices substitute other names for those of their comrades. Only the luckless sans "protection" were taken. The doctors examined the selectees to determine their fitness for travel; the rabbis gave quick divorces so that Jewish women would not have the uncertain religious status of deserted wives; the employment office checked the registration cards; the Jewish police kept order in the ranks of the deportees as they marched to the railway station where the Germans took over. Rumkowski assured the Jews left behind that the deportees were going out to places where they would do agricultural work. At the loading platforms there were no bloody scenes, as in Warsaw; all went smoothly. The deportations started on January 15 and ended on January 29, 1942, when the quota was reached. A total of 10,103 was sent out "for resettlement." The deportees reached their final destination at Chelmno. None returned.

That was only a beginning. Chelmno could not remain idle. The Germans ignored the promise they had made to Rumkowski. They had an efficient system in operation, inside the ghetto as well as without, and they took good advantage of it. "Resettlement" resumed. The Germans encouraged voluntary enlistment for deportation by arbitrarily cutting down the rations for the ghetto, thus increasing the hunger and persuading the Jews they would be better off anywhere else than in Litzmannstadt. Biebow was unconcerned about the killing of the Jews, but he worried that his profits would drop. He protested that productivity was being impaired. "The health of the Jews sinks daily because the official rations exist only on paper, no food being allowed to come into the ghetto. . . . The best proof of the nutritional status is the rapidly rising mortality rate. For example, from February 22 to February 26, 74 persons died of pulmonary tuberculosis, 105 from heart failure, 84 from undernutrition—better called starvation, and 44 from various causes all traceable to malnutrition. . . ." His superiors ignored Biebow. They were less interested in productivity than in getting rid of the Jews once and for all. Between February 22 and April 2, 34,073 more had been "resettled." On April 18, Rumkowski ordered all the unemployed over ten years of age to report for examination by a German medical commission to determine their fitness for work. That was a sign that new deportations were at hand, but this time Rumkowski managed to get rid of disturbing elements in "his ghetto," the Western European Jews.

Between May 4 and May 15, only 753 Lodz Jews ("criminals" and volunteers) were deported. The rest of the transports was made up of 10,161 Western European Jews, almost all of those left after the deaths from sickness and starvation. Exempted were doctors and nurses, employees of the ghetto administration, holders of the Iron Cross, and those wounded in the German army in World War I. No resistance to the deportations was offered; apathy was the mood of the Western European Jews. "Sooner or later," they said, "we'd be deported. Better to go out with our own kind rather than with the *Ostjuden*." Many German Jews in the exempt classes volunteered to go; they wanted to die in their Fatherland (where they thought they were going) rather than in the hell of the ghetto. The Germans paid their Jewish compatriots an honor: every deportee had a reserved seat in a third-class carriage.

Many of the "old inhabitants" felt the same way as Rumkowski about the departure of the Western European Jews. One diarist wrote sarcastically, apropos of that attitude: "In the new selections [for deportation] the President shot two birds with one bullet: he got rid of unproductive human material and dispensed justice. . . . His people were brothers, the others stepbrothers. They couldn't even understand the language of the ghetto. Besides that, most of them were old, and those that weren't were hopeless of assimilation. . . . When it came to a choice, the President had to keep his productive element. . . . Who can criticize a good father who supports his own darlings with all his strength?"

Rumkowski felt his stable ghetto getting shaky. To placate the workers he ordered extra cigarette rations to be given out. And to insure that that would not be misunderstood as a sign of the weakening of his power, he abolished the Summary Courts and personally took over their functions. To compensate for the irregular provisioning, he urged the gardeners in Marysin to expand their farm work. He feared that more deportations might come. On July 20, 1942, he ordered that all children over ten years of age must go to work. About 13,000 were found places in the factories. Those over seventeen were treated as adults. Those from ten to seventeen worked shorter hours, had special supervision to see that they bathed and had their hair cut (to prevent lousiness and thus typhus fever), and had medical and dental care available at the factories. Rumkowski, watchful as ever over his beloved children, saw to it that a mobile library went from workshop to workshop to satisfy the youngsters' craving for reading matter.

Hunger spread. The summer of 1942 saw a further reduction in rations so that the average worker got only 1,100 calories daily if he worked full time. Orders from German firms, moreover, were being cut down because of the expected imminent extermination of the Jews. With fewer orders and lessened total productivity came another decrease in the provisioning of the ghetto. Rumkowski shut his eyes to the diabolical cause of the spreading starvation. He blamed the watery soup served in the kitchens on thieving kitchen personnel. To show his concern for the workers, he took advantage of the smaller workload and decreed that cottages in the Marysin area be set aside as seven-day vacation spots for workers. The vacations were not obligatory; they could be traded for extra rations. Most of the workers chose the extra rations. The cottages were occupied by the bureaucrats. Rumkowski's own summer house was ironically called by the ghetto dwellers "Tsarskoye Selo," the name of the former Tsar's summer palace.

Since he could not supply food, the least Rumkowski felt he could do was to try to improve the social services. He proclaimed, "As the ghetto population knows full well, I want to keep improving the health status of the people and I want to do justice to all"—by fixing the fees doctors could charge: three marks for an office visit, five for a house call, and seven for a consultation.

And to show his concern for productivity, Rumkowski issued an order on August 20, 1942, that anyone who stole any article from a workshop or factory would be severely punished by solitary confinement in prison, and that anyone who knew of such thefts and did not inform the plant manager of them would be treated as an accomplice and would get the same punishment.

The summer passed quietly, but then another blow came to the ghetto. On September 1, with the aid of the Jewish police, the Germans cleaned out the hospitals. Early on that morning, trucks drove up to their doors. SS men blocked the adjoining streets and ordered the directors to empty out the hospitals within ten minutes. The evacuation was brutal. Any patient who protested or even asked a question was shot on the spot, as were relatives who broke through the police lines, pleading to say a last farewell to their loved ones. In several cases, the Germans maliciously allowed parents to join their children or vice versa and then loaded them together on the trucks. Some patients succeeded in escaping in the confusion, and fled to their homes; among these were 130 from the Mieckiewicz Street hospital. Within two hours, five hospitals were totally cleared out; 2,000 patients, including 400 children, were taken away.

The tragedy did not end there. The Germans checked the hospital registers, decided that a large number of patients were missing, and ordered them delivered up for deportation. Searches were made in the homes of their closest relatives; when the missing patients were not found, hostages were taken in their place so that the quota would be completed. Another of Rumkowski's slogans, "Care for the Sick," now lost all meaning.

Immediately afterward came the edict of horror, for which the ghetto blamed Rumkowski. They said that he had convinced the Germans that the productive ghetto Jews were necessary for the German war economy; the Germans went one step further and decided that no other Jews were. An order came that 20,000 more were to be deported—in inhumanly special categories: all children under ten and all adults over sixty-five, 17,000 in all, plus 3,000 unemployed or unemployable. Exempted were the children of the administrative personnel, including the police and fire brigades.

Rumkowski's speech announcing the decree was both heart-rending and self-justifying. "The ghetto has received a hard blow. They ask of us the best we have—children and old people. I never had the luck to have a child of my own and so I gave up the best years of my life to children. . . . In my old age I must stretch out my hands and beg, 'Brothers and sisters, give them to me! Fathers and mothers, give me your children!'. . . . Yesterday I received an order to send some 21,000 Jews out of the ghetto. 'If you don't do it, we will.' And the question arose, 'Should we do it or leave it to others?' Even more important is the question of not how many will we lose but of how many can we save? We all, myself and my closest associates, have come to the conclusion that despite the horrible responsibility, we have to accept the evil order. I have to perform this bloody operation myself; I have to cut off limbs to save the body! I have to take away the children, because otherwise others will also be taken, God forbid! . . . Look at me! My whole life was bound up with the welfare of children and the care of the sick, and now I can't even help my own relatives! . . . I tried to save the nine-year-olds at least, but they say no . . . We have in the ghetto many people .

sick with tuberculosis whose lives are numbered in weeks, perhaps in days. I do not know—perhaps this is a fiendish idea, and again perhaps it is not—but I can't help mentioning it. Deliver to me those sick people and maybe I'll be able to save the healthy. . . It's better to get rid of those with only days or weeks to live than to send out healthy people who earn us the bread we need. Those others don't get better and we get sick. . . . We'll feed the swine with the sick. . . . I stand before you a broken-down Jew. Don't envy me. This is the worst task I've ever undertaken. I stretch out my weak, trembling hands to you, and I plead—give me those victims to forestall their demand for more victims, to save a hundred thousand Jews. . . . That's what they told me—give up the victims yourselves and all will be peaceful once more." He was interrupted by wailing and cries of "We'll all go!" and "Mr. President! Exempt one-child families and take only from those with several children!" Rumkowski became angry. He shouted, "That's all idle talk! I have no strength to enter into debates with you! If some German official came, you wouldn't cry out! I begged yesterday on my knees to no avail! Just remember—from the villages of seven and eight thousand Jews, barely a thousand came here, so what's better? What do you want? Eighty or ninety thousand left behind, or all wiped out? Condemn whom you will, only save the remaining Jews. I'm not talking to hotheads. I appeal to your understanding and common sense. I've done everything and I'll do everything to prevent guns from being used in the ghetto and to keep blood from being spilled. We can't go against the order, only lighten its execution. Do you think the Germans will be so gentle and kind if they carry out the order themselves?"

Rumkowski was correct in his estimate of the Germans. The children from the orphan asylums were peacefully removed, but the Jewish police were too slow with the rounding-up process in individual families. They could not cope with the resistance they met. The Germans took charge. With typical bestiality, besides children and old people, they seized others at random—for gray hair, for too short a stature, for too many wrinkles. The noise of gunfire resounded in the ghetto. From September 5th to the 12th, 15,589 had been deported and about 600 shot on the spot. Hans Biebow, the "humanitarian" who had asked for more food for the Jews under his rule, was in charge of the action.

8

Rumkowski, like the other Jews, was saddened by the loss of the children, but, unlike the others, he lost no faith in the soundness of his plans for the ghetto. He rode around again, blaming the ghetto Jews for not beliving him when he had preached that work was their only salvation. He protected the remaining children by making them work in the shops, even those nine-year-olds who had been exempted from deportation because they belonged to the privileged bureacracy. He ordered the parents of those younger than nine to take them to their places of employment where day care would be provided while their parents worked. Twenty percent of the labor force was made up of minors up to the age of seventeen. Gone were the schools and the orphan asylums together with the other philanthropic institutions; their buildings were used for new factories. The machines whirred faster. Nobody dared to grumble' about working conditions. The workers hated Rumkowski but were forced to admit that his "work policy" had saved them from the unknown fate of the deported Jews. As Rumkowski had said, a work card meant life, the hope of survival.

No news of the killings at Chelmno filtered into the ghetto. And no word came from the deportees. Rumkowski tried to evade answering questions. At a meeting he was asked what had happened to those who had been deported. He replied testily, "I wasn't there. I don't know if they're still living or already in the Other World. They don't tell me what They did with the selected Jews. When I tell Them we don't have any more sick Jews in the ghetto, They just laugh at me. We have to pray to God that the war will soon end because the longer it lasts, the worse it gets for us. Don't ask any more questions and don't push for answers.

Just do your work quietly." Rumkowski's words indicated he was beginning to doubt the truth of what his German overlords told him. The Jews shuddered and followed his advice.

They had good reason to shudder. In October, eleven relatives and friends of David Gertler, the head of the Special Division of the Jewish police, came from Warsaw by special arrangement with the Germans. The eleven told of the tremendous mass evacuations there that had reduced the ghetto population to a tenth of its former number. Although they said their information was uncertain, they believed that the evacuees had been killed, as indeed they had been, at Treblinka.

Despite his exalted position in the ghetto, Rumkowski himself was no better off than any other Jew when he displeased a member of the Master Race. Biebow, drunk, swaggered into Rumkowski's office one day and, because of a trivial misunderstanding, beat him up so severely that he had to be hospitalized.

The German race madness was noted in a police report of October 21, 1942, in which, replying to a request from the authorities, the police solemnly stated that a thorough investigation had revealed that in the ghetto there were no Negroes or mulattoes!

The food supply still remained the major problem of the ghetto. Biebow again argued with his superiors for more food "because even of the official quota little is sent in . . . Despite the last evacuation in September . . . 4,658 died from then up to March 31, 1943. Malnutrition will necessarily increase. . . . Jews get much less than the Poles who produce less . . ." His arguments did no good.

Rumkowski lost many of his ideas about an autonomous Jewish enclave. All his efforts were now directed to propitiating the Germans so that his ghetto would remain untouched. He went out of his way to anticipate their demands. Two examples: Instead of secretly taking part of the personal property left behind by the deportees for communal use, he had it carefully inventoried and stored until the Germans were ready to appropriate it. And his police rigidly enforced all German orders to the extent of turning over to the German guards a man who was found not wearing the Jewish badge.

Rumkowski's belief that, such sacrifices having been made to the German Moloch, the rest of the ghetto would stay intact was fostered by the elimination of the Deportation Commission. His belief was shared by other Jews. The semiofficial *Ghetto Chronicle* reported, "Great joy in the ghetto population because of the news that by a statement of the highest officials in Berlin the ghetto will be regarded as a labor camp. It is hoped, therefore, that following this there will be an improvement in our living conditions and provisioning."

Orders came in. Workshops became factories organized on assembly lines. Over 7,000 sewing machines were in use. On December 12, 1942, Rumkowski made a speech in which he said, "Our children and our children's children will proudly remember the names of all those who contributed to the creation of the most important Jewish achievement in the ghetto: the labor opportunities that granted *Lebensrecht* [the right to live]." In another talk he said, "We live by virtue of this production and by this alone."

The ghetto was at relative peace in 1943, although two deportations (of 950 and 500 Jews in March and August, respectively) took place. The Jews heard through the hidden radios of the defeat at Stalingrad, of the fighting in Africa, of the Russian advances. The news had its effect. Hopes of early liberation rose, and feeble attempts at sabotage occurred in the form of ca' canny (*pracuj powoli,* in Polish, meaning "work slowly"). More than once, Rumkowski thundered at the slackers who jeopardized the safety of the ghetto and at the rumor-mongers who spread false tales of an early German collapse. He worried that productivity would decline. He got new contracts with private German firms eager to profit from the slave labor of the Jews, but Biebow, who got no rake-off from such contracts, soon put a stop to that. Rumkowski then turned in another direction to increase productivity. He rationalized factory techniques and developed new consumer industries for the Reich home front as well as expanded production for the *Wehrmacht.* Transmission belts were made from bits of leather, rubber, and torn knapsacks; toys were made of papiermâché; bloody uniforms from the Eastern Front were cleaned and repaired.

His influence was waning, however. The Special Division of the police, headed by David Gertler, was now in charge of food distribution. That function had been taken away from Rumkowski by Biebow in retaliation for the signs of Rumkowski's "independence." But Rumkowski was needed, if only as the titular head of the ghetto. Biebow felt it necessary to call a meeting of the factory representatives in the ghetto to tell them that they should obey Rumkowski, the Eldest of the Jews, because "he had the full authority over them." Rumkowski himself was compelled to change his tone. Gone was his claim of infallibility. Instead, in a speech to workshop leaders, he complained, "If I've made mistakes, I'm only human. You should have pointed out my errors to me."

By the end of 1943, 79,648 Jews were left in the ghetto. More than 85 percent were working for German industry, producing goods to the value of 27,000,000 Reichsmarks. The Jews, who had heard stories of mass killings, did not believe them, dismissing them as part of the German terror-propaganda machine to keep the Jews in submission. The Jews were logical. They knew that the Germans would not impair the war economy by destroying an essential part of it—the labor of the Jews. The Jews calculated the cost of deporting so many Jews from Litzmannstadt and the number of trains needed, and they came to the conclusion that such a deportation was impossible. They generally agreed that Rumkowski's "work policy" had paid off. Rumkowski was no good, of course, but one had to give him credit in this case. Regarding the deportees, the general feeling was that they had been herded together somewhere in Eastern Europe on reservations like the American Indian reservations.

The people worked and grumbled and hungered. Provisioning, previously so limited in amount, was suddenly increased in August, so that the High Holy Days were well celebrated. For the first time Rumkowski permitted the workers to have a half-holiday on New Year's Day; to fool the Germans they went to their factories as usual but they did no work. Yom Kippur was a total day of rest—it fell on a Sunday. Rumkowski lifted his head a little bit. He said the greater provisioning was a reward for the ghetto's greater productivity.

Perhaps it was. Or perhaps it was a bone thrown to forestall such an uprising as had occurred in Warsaw. The difficulty in suppressing that revolt of the doomed had sent shivers of shock through the ranks of the Germans in Berlin. The military situation was too precarious to have to divert troops to Litzmannstadt. Although their informers told them that no resistance was contemplated, the Germans took no chances.

The Ghetto of Lodz now remained the only ghetto in Poland. All the others had been liquidated. Effectively sealed off as it was, the outside world could only guess what went on in it. The underground Jewish National Committee made several attempts to gain entry into it or to send messages to it, warning the Jews of their impending fate. Their attempts being unsuccessful, the Committee enlisted the aid of the Polish underground, with equal lack of success. In a letter to Switzerland the Jewish National Committee reported on May 24, 1944, "Lodz is an island, isolated from the rest of the world."

Early in 1944 Rumkowski transmitted the German order to close down some of the shops and see that the workers volunteered for deportation. He found no ready compliance as in the past. Even the hell of Lodz was better, the workers reasoned, than the uncertainties of "resettlement," especially now that the secret radio was carrying reports of German defeats, and the end of the war was imminent. Rumkowski resorted to his old weapon: he cut off rations for the workers in the closed factories. He encouraged his police to search for those who failed to show up for deportation and to take their wives in their stead. Hunger broke down the weak passive resistance. Substitutes for deportation were easily procurable—for two loaves of bread and a kilogram of sugar.

Rumkowski used all his powers of persuasion to assure the workers that deportation did not necessarily mean death. He was helped by the classic German perfidy: postcards from the "resettled," careful labeling of baggage to avoid misdirection, advice on what to take. Rumkowski unwittingly aided the deception. He set up a special department to buy the household goods of those scheduled for deportation; the price was paid in Reichsmarks, not in Rumkes; some was given immediately so that the workers would have spending money available when they reached Germany (the supposed destination); the rest was placed on deposit "for their account when they return." Rumkowski went about urging people to volunteer for the transports, saying that workers were needed in Germany to replace the Germans taken for the army. He also warned that the Russians, if they reached Lodz, would not be merciful to the Jews who had worked so faithfully for the Nazis for five long years.

Ghetto life was smashed in every direction. Rumkowski's pride, the bank, was liquidated. His administrative personnel was cut down. His accounting department was closed. Fewer and fewer orders for manufactured goods came in, and Germans began to demand the return of unworked-on raw materials. Even then Rumkowski desperately tried to maintain his "productive ghetto." He told the doctors, "Times have gotten worse here. We live under orders and those orders must be carried out. . . . Understand what's happening! . . . Don't cut down productivity by giving out too many excuses from work for sickness! . . ."

In March of 1944 the entire Chancellery was closed except for an office to be used by Rumkowski. The bureaucrats who had lived so well before in comparison with the mass of the ghetto population were sent to do hard physical labor in razing houses near the ghetto borders and in building new barracks near the railroad station in Marysin.

In April the ghetto was reduced in size, and rations were cut down. More deportations were ordered, but more passive resistance in the form of hiding took place. The ghetto population had heard of the German defeats on all fronts. Demonstrations in the factories and go-slow strikes caused Rumkowski to exclaim on one occasion, "Against whom are you demonstrating—against me? I'm only a servant of the authorities and must also bend my head and be obedient." He worried about the presence of the few remaining children on the streets and ordered all, regardless of age, to be taken into the factories.

On June 7, 1944, after the secret radio listeners had spread the word of D-Day, the Kripo swooped down on several groups who had been receiving Allied broadcasts. The ghetto shivered. What vengeance, what collective punishment would the Nazis mete out for such flagrant violation of their decrees?

Nothing happened. Mildness became the tone of the Germans, a mildness that was taken as a sign by the people that German defeat was imminent.

Rumkowski was now only a figurehead, disregarded both by the Germans and the Jews. The insurance agent who had risen to be an "exalted eminence," the Eldest of the Jews, was a pathetic old man mouthing the phrases of his past glory. The Jews no longer listened to him. Better sounds than his advice were in their ears—the artillery of the Red Army in the distance. The Jews saw the Soviet airplanes overhead. They learned that the liberators were nearing the gates of Warsaw. "Almost! Almost!" was the cry. "Only a few days more!"

And with hope went talk, alas! only talk, of passive resistance, of hiding until the Germans left Lodz. Work absenteeism increased to such an extent that Rumkowski took note of it. He went about making speeches about the declining productivity in the factories and ranted about "wicked elements that until now have stayed in the background." His words had little effect.

The German extermination process did not slow down. Order for deportation followed order. Slowly, slowly the ghetto was emptied out, but with increasing resistance. Rumkowski repeated what had been told him—more workers were needed in Germany to clear away the debris of Allied bombardments and to take the place in the factories of the German reserves called up for military dut . The Jews paid little attention to him. They went to the trains now only by force.

In August, 1944, came the final decree only a short time after Biebow had given Rumkowski his word that the Ghetto of Litzmannstadt would not be "resettled." Orders came to liquidate all the ghetto enterprises and arrange to send the workers "elsewhere." No selection would be made. Entire factories with their workers and their families were to go. Rumkowski still cooperated with the Germans even though his authority would end with the end of the ghetto. The habit of obedience to German commands and the impetus given him by his past actions carried him on. He told the ghetto workers to go peaceably, otherwise the Germans would use force and they knew what that meant. One of his last orders, dated August 24, 1944, told the ghetto inhabitants to make sure that all the electric lights were turned off in the homes and factories they left, so that Allied planes would not be led to bomb Lodz.

Seven hundred men and women were left behind in the ghetto as clean-up gangs. They were mostly intellectuals under the special protection of Rumkowski. He could have stayed behind with them, but he chose not to. Did he believe the German lies that the Jews were going out to a new work area? Or did he feel that his place was with "his Jews" and that he must stay at his post to do his duty as their leader? Rumkowski, seeing his brother and his family going on the last train on August 30, 1944, asked to leave with them, to leave Lodz for the common terminus of the final contingent—Auschwitz. (Chelmno was no longer functioning.) At Auschwitz he received his ultimate honor from the Germans. They conducted him to a small hill from which he could see "his Jews" march past him to the gas chambers. He joined them at the end of the line.

9

Rumkowski, in his blind self-conceit, never considered his reign threatened by any other individual. He felt he had the ear of Biebow. Biebow, for his own interests, although he knew that the deportees were not being resettled but were going to the death camps, fostered Rumkowski's illusion that the Jews could survive by working faithfully for the Germans. He thus encouraged Rumkowski's fond idea that in a special sense he and Biebow were partners. But when Rumkowski seemed to be getting too independent, Biebow had no hesitation in cutting him down. Biebow had other Jews he could count on.

The most important of those Jews was David Gertler, the head of the Special Division, a police department. The Special Division was both a political and an economic agency. Its function was to inform Rumkowski of activities subversive of him and of the German rulers, to abort attempts at resistance, and to uncover for confiscation any hidden Jewish assets in the ghetto in the form of goods or valuables. Before the war and the occupation, Gertler had been a secret police agent for the Polish internal revenue service; his job then was to ferret out materials on which no tax had been paid. Under the Nazis he became a trusted Gestapo agent. As head of the Special Division he had many opportunities to keep his superiors well informed about the situation in the ghetto.

It was probably Gertler who had made the Gestapo aware of the illegal activities of his nominal chief, Solomon Hertzberg. Hertzberg had been appropriating for his own use part of the goods and valuables left behind by the deported Jews early in 1942. He was arrested and sent off to Chelmno.

Gertler then let it be known in the ghetto that because of his good connections he could arrange for Jews to leave Lodz for Warsaw "for a price." A number of Jews (187) actually reached that destination after paying him off.

To show Rumkowski that his rule depended on him and that no independent actions were permissible (such as arranging for private contracts), Biebow put Gertler in charge of the very important Provisioning Office, bypassing Rumkowski's authority completely. Gertler immediately instituted "reforms" to ingratiate himself with the ghetto population: he abolished the special supplements for Rumkowski's favorites and he distributed all food sent in instead of maintaining reserves that too often rotted in storage, thus convincing the people that he was a better administrator than Rumkowski. He also took credit for the cessation of the deportations, and many Jews believed him.

The Gestapo, whose man Gertler was, would have liked to put him at the head of the Jewish community, but Biebow was unwilling to go so far. Rumkowski, through his bureaucracy, still held the important industrial power. Officially, Biebow supported Rumkowski as the sole authority; unofficially he helped the growth of Gertler's power. Gertler took on the role of saving individuals from Rumkowski's punishments. And like The Thirteeners' gang in Warsaw, he publicly vowed to stop malversation of food products (especially bread). The Special Division took over supervision of the large bakeries.

Rumkowski saw his power being threatened. The big talker now kept silent, but he bided his time. In March of 1943 he uncovered corruption and embezzlement in Gertler's bakery inspectors. Although Gertler still remained in control of provisioning, his popular image was damaged. Furthermore, the despoliation of the Jews now being complete, no valuables being left to be uncovered, his Special Division men were reduced to acting as auxiliary police and as political spies among the Jews.

On July 13, 1943, Gertler suddenly disappeared from the ghetto. His deputy, Klieger, took his place. Wild speculations arose about Gertler's whereabouts. He was not heard from again until he surfaced after the war as a witness in a war crimes trial in the American Zone of Germany. He said he had been a prisoner in Auschwitz, kept from death by some of his former comrades. They hid him in a special solitary cell, provided him with food and water, and later wangled for him a soft job as a storeroom clerk in the Buna factory attached to Auschwitz. In 1960 he was reported to be a wealthy manufacturer in West Germany. In 1973 he was said to own a chain of factories across Western Europe.

10

No organized resistance movement against the Germans or against Rumkowski as the transmitter of German orders ever developed in the Lodz Ghetto, as it did in Warsaw and Vilna. Little opportunity existed for resistance. The Judenrat of Litzmannstadt, elsewhere more or less distortedly representative of the Jewish community, was a paper organization; the leadership principle exemplified in Rumkowski's person was paramount. His "national-socialism" and his bureaucracy reached into every nook and cranny of ghetto life. Elsewhere the Jews saw the Germans as the cause of their troubles; in Litzmannstadt they saw only the dictator Rumkowski and were powerless before him.

For a short period before the 1940 strikes and demonstrations, the proletarian parties (Bund, Right and Left Labor Zionists, Communists) got together in a United Front to coordinate their activities. Rumkowski used their hunger and ration cards to break down morale. They had no underground press to stimulate the ghetto to action. Their most effectual efforts were in support of comrades punished by Rumkowski and later in their maneuverings to save them from deportation.

The political leaders (except for some Young Zionists) felt that an organized armed resistance was hopeless. No weapons were available or procurable. Unarmed resistance by weak and starving Jews was a dangerous dream, they reasoned, one that could only end in total destruction of the ghetto and its inhabitants.

Help from the Polish underground was out of the question. The anti-Semitic program of the prewar Polish government had had its effect on the working class. Anti-Semitism, although officially proscribed by the underground Polish working-class parties, was almost ingrained in their members, and the German hate-propaganda undoubtedly had strengthened that feeling. Furthermore, after the Germans took over Lodz, many of the Poles were sent as slave labor to Germany and most of the remaining Poles were moved to an area of the city far removed from the ghetto; contact between radical Jews and Poles became impossible. The Left Union (Communists) in the ghetto were in the same position vis-à-vis their Polish counterparts as the Bundist socialists were with theirs. In addition, those few Poles who had declared themselves Volksdeutsche but who tried to make contact with the political parties in the ghetto were justifiably regarded with suspicion as agents-provocateurs.

Individuals who by active or passive opposition (refusal to pay rent, arguments with the Jewish police, failure to report for work, etc.) tried to counteract Rumkowski's orders were quickly taken care of by arrest and imprisonment. The resistance of parents against the deportation of their children was bloodily suppressed by the Germans.

Whatever murmurings took place were whispered for fear of Rumkowski's heavy hand. A few satirical poems were circulated in the workshops. One went:

> I am a policeman
> With a special talent—
> To yell around Rumkowski,
> Bully with all my strength,
> Eat until I burst. . . .

Several hidden radio sets served as nuclei for tiny circles that spread the news gleaned from Allied broadcasts. The largest circle was that of Dr. Daniel Weiskop. Unfortunately, as the existentialist philosophers say, no man knows the consequences of his actions. The disseminators of the news reports served to hold back resistance by bolstering the optimism of the masses that soon Hitler would be defeated, the war would be over, and they would be freed.

By 1943, after the deportations, Rumkowski's plan for a "productive ghetto" seemed to be a success. Food supplies got better; cultural activities and study circles took on new life. A few "military groups" were formed, groups that studied the art of warfare from books. Such activities were regarded by older and wiser heads as silly. The groups soon ceased to exist.

Furthermore, the number of political activists was small. Of the about 68,000 Jews in Litzmannstadt, the Bund had 935 members, the Zionist Pioneer groups 1,000, the Communists 1,500. The number of adherents to other parties is not known, but it is supposed that the most generous estimate of all parties combined had to be less than 5,000.

In 1944, after the Allies had landed in Normandy, the end of the war seemed near. Most of the Jews reasoned, "Why fight now and get killed when we've survived so long?" And Rumkowski was still able to convince others that the removal of the Jews from the ghetto was to work camps in Germany.

At this time, when the ghetto was beginning to be liquidated, a debate arose in the Communist movement, an ironic debate in view of what happened later. A group of Young Communists wanted to start fires in the factories and commit other acts of sabotage. Their older comrades prevailed on them not to do so on the ground that the factories should be delivered intact in the near future when the "people's authority" would take over.

From all the documents available, we know that Rumkowski himself never once mentioned armed or unarmed resistance to the Germans, even at the bitter end. He evidently felt the subject was not worthy of discussion.

11

The memoirs, the diaries, the archives of the Ghetto of Litzmannstadt depict the ambiguous attitudes of the Jews toward Rumkowski. Sometimes he was applauded for his efforts to maintain the ghetto as a safe haven for the Jews, but most often he was condemned as an out-and-out villain. Here is a sampling of comments about him from those who were there:

Jonah Shulman, a teacher: He was confident that his name would go down in history. Even before the closed ghetto, he believed he was destined for an exalted mission. He was a sick and weak man, but now he stopped worrying about his health. All along, his eyes were fixed on his goal—the welfare of all Israel [the Jews]. Indeed, ambition for power was not the major factor in his activities, but slowly, slowly, his ideals faded and the desire to rule got stronger.

Karo, the secretary of the gymnasium: What can I say—that all that the President does is fine and kosher? I can't say that, but neither can I say that everything that he does is bad. Actually he desires that everything should go well with the Jews in the ghetto, and furthermore, he doesn't want all his plans to go for naught. To tell the truth, he bears no blame at all. He is merely the one who carries out the orders of Biebow and his associates. One error indeed he makes—a great one, and that is that he won't learn. He says he understands everything, and at a time when life and death hang by a hair his plans can't be carried out. Everything that he does has to be done with a strong hand; if not, the ghetto people would eat each other alive. He tried to use various methods in building up the workshops. And what happened then? They stole right and left, they didn't follow instructions at work, they made light of his orders. He came to the conclusion, therefore, that he would listen to no one and with an iron hand he alone would carry out all the orders given him.

Bernard Freund, the ex-president of the Craftsmen's Union: I don't blame Rumkowski. He doesn't abide by all his declarations and undertakings, but we must say that were it not for Rumkowski and his strong hand the Jewish community of Lodz would long ago have been destroyed. It's clear that the Germans wanted at the outset to wipe out the whole of Lodz Jewry. They didn't want to make a ghetto in Lodz. They wanted to deport all the Jews to Bedzin and there carry out their dark plans. The thought of making a ghetto, which came from Rumkowski, made it possible for the Lodz Jews to stay at least for a while in one place and get food and work. It's true that from time to time people were torn from their families and homes, but on the whole the Lodz community was not touched. Unfortunately we had no other choice. The enemy wanted to exterminate us. He didn't hide his intentions. He needed, however, cheap work hands, and who else could he take but the Jews? Not Rumkowski, not his police, not those who work under Rumkowski bear the responsibility. We were condemned to destruction by the Germans. The world would have forgotten us . . . We must work and keep quiet, not arouse the wolf to destroy us . . . We can't count on the outside world because they don't know what's happening here and they're not interested in our sufferings.

The folklorist Shkepitzk: The children sing, "Rumkowski the good, give us food." Much better it would have been were he to give us poison. He was a bastard even in the days of his orphan asylum when the world was still normal. It is sad that our Jews should permit such a sadist to carry out the extermination of Lodz Jewry.

The journalist Rosenstein: Nobody in Lodz could take the wheel of such a hell-ship as well as Rumkowski . . . If we had more popular leaders with a sense of brotherhood at the head, we'd have been better off . . . I don't think Rumkowski knows about all that goes on. He's between the hammer and the anvil. He can't do differently than what he does except commit suicide. Such an act is not for him. Rumkowski loves life, he loves power, and he'll do anything to keep the power in his hands.

Engineer Feifel, a leftist: I once thought Rumkowski was a good man, but the more I knew him, the more I realized he was the factor that caused our sorrow . . . He was a disturber of the peace, an abortion of nature. What Hitler says is right: the Jews cause their own destruction when you see traitors, bandits, and bastards like him. . . . Rumkowski and his clique are our misfortune.

Jack Moss, a survivor, member of the final clean-up squad: Rumkowski was a foolish, vain, conceited man. Yet I must admit he had principles. . . . One had to be crazy as he was, an unbounded egotist, to shoulder such a job as he had. . . .

12

Rumkowski, the blustering autocrat, presents the psychologic picture of overcompensation for inferiority, real or imagined. He was raised in poverty in a society where wealth offered the only opportunity to escape from anti-Semitic restrictions. His education was limited, but his milieu honored the learned. He was a widower and had no children to carry on his name. He struggled for material success, only to be beaten down by circumstances.

Yet Rumkowski had forces within him that fought hard against his background and his ill-fortune. If he could no longer be a wealthy industrialist and a "big giver" to charity, then he would show his philanthropy in other ways. If he was childless, then he would be a surrogate father to orphans. If he was a widower, then he would remarry—and marry a woman much younger than himself and with higher education.

But it was the chance that made him "the Eldest of the Jews of Litzmannstadt" that gave him the opportunity to demonstrate his worth to the world—his world, the Jewish community. Now he could show the intellectuals who had sneered at him and the rich who had pitied him that Mordecai Chaim Rumkowski was a great man. He would be a Samson among the Philistines, he would outshine all the Court Jews of history, he would be another Moses.

Nevertheless, underneath the loud voice and the arrogant phrases lurked the feeling that he was actually unequal to the task before him. Unwilling to admit such a possibility, he became evermore convinced that he and he alone knew what was best to do. An admirable compensation for inferiority changed into an undesirable overcompensation and ultimately into an almost mad desire to rule.

The Germans stood in the way of absolute rule, but Rumkowski closed his eyes to that fact. He deluded himself with Messianic visions. His megalomania coincided with the need of the Germans for a strong authority over the Jews. It blinded him to the consequences of his actions.

13

It is too facile to label Rumkowski as a lunatic with the fixed idea that he was fated to save the Jews from destruction. Then what else can we say of him from our vantage point of another time and another place? What can we say of a man who loved children and who cooperated in their deportation to an end he knew could only be death? Of a man no longer in the prime of life who sacrificed other old men and women to save the young to work for the Germans? Of a sentimental holiday-Jew who had his police cut off beards and earlocks lest his masters be offended? Of a former businessman who organized a "national commune?" What can we say of one whose Messianic dream became a nightmare for the Jews? Dare we say—"He meant well?"

Ironically enough, Rumkowski's policy of accommodation and saving the Jews by having them work for the Germans might have succeeded. Lodz was the last of the ghettos to be liquidated. Already in the summer of 1944 the Soviet army was rolling the Nazis back through Poland. The Volksdeutsche and the erstwhile conquerors from the General-Gouvernement were fleeing through the streets of Lodz. Had the Red Army kept up the initial momentum of its summer offensive (it stopped only seventy-five miles from Lodz), tens of thousands of Jews in Lodz would have been rescued. Rumkowski then could truly have claimed to have been the "Savior of the Jews." A dead savior, for the surviving Jews would undoubtedly have torn him limb from limb in furious revenge for their sufferings under his rule.

Chairman Adam Czerniakow

On September 17, 1940, Chaim A. Kaplan, a principal of a Hebrew school, made a cynical commentary in his diary about the rumor that Czerniakow, the head of the Warsaw Judenrat, had committed suicide:

> To the experts, the entire story seemed unlikely. First, whoever heard of a clever public official doing something so stupid? Our public servants may be accused of anything but love for the Jews. It is very doubtful whether Czerniakow's worry and pain over the general misfortune are so great as to be heartbreaking, let alone bring him to a state of general depression so deep that he would commit suicide. As to Czerniakow himself, he is a mediocre man whose intelligence and education combine to make him something of a nincompoop; it is only through the bad luck of his people that he has risen to such eminence. Never before has he been so successful as in these evil hours . . .
>
> So praise the Lord! "Our" Czerniakow is still alive. As to

the seventeen edicts, nothing is known clearly; but if, heaven forbid, they are enacted, Czerniakow will assist in carrying them out, and his heart will not break, nor will he commit suicide.

1

German planes bombarded Warsaw from the very first day of the war, September 1, 1939. The speed with which the Panzer divisions swept across Poland, city after city falling before their onslaught, and the rapid disintegration of the Polish army led the Germans to believe that the Polish government would soon collapse and the capital fall into their hands without too much trouble. Within a week the Germans were at the outskirts of Warsaw.

To the Nazis' surprise and annoyance, Warsaw was defended as other Polish cities were not. Warsaw's mayor, Stefan Starzyński, called on its inhabitants to resist, to build barricades and trenches, to fight street by street, house by house. The initial German offensive was slowed up; German infantry could not advance. Heavy artillery bombardment of the city was now added to the air raids. Still the city held out. Stragglers from the Polish army, who had made their way to Warsaw, were regrouped. More than 150,000 troops faced the enemy.

On September 17, the Soviet Union invaded eastern Poland. The next day President Ignace Moscicki and Field Marshal Smigly-Ridz, the commander of the army, fled to Romania. No Polish government remained. Nevertheless, besieged as no other capital city had been in modern times, Warsaw still fought on.

Its surrender, despite the exhortations of the mayor, was only a matter of time. No food could come into the city. Gas and electricity connections were cut off by bombs. The telephone exchange was demolished. Sewage from the blasted sewers fouled the streets already cluttered with the bodies of dead horses and human beings. A bomb made a direct hit on the main water pumping station; most of Warsaw lost its drinking water. A few wells on the outskirts and the Vistula River were the only sources of water, and the queues that formed to get water became the object of low-flying German strafing planes.

Finally, on September 27, the senior army officer in the capital, General Julius Rommel, ordered the surrender of the 140,000 officers and men under his command. The German infantry marched in triumphantly.

The prewar Jewish population of Warsaw numbered about 300,000. It had increased to almost half a million because of the influx of refugees fleeing from the advancing German army. After the surrender of the city, as in Lodz, the Jews were subjected to hooligan attacks by German soldiers and by anti-Semitic Poles who blamed the Jews for being the cause of the national misfortune. Jews were pulled out of lines waiting at the emergency soup kitchens; they were openly robbed and beaten on the streets; they were forced into humiliating and degrading tasks for the amusement of the conquerors.

The city had to be cleared of the rubble and devastation caused by the bombings. Who could do that better than the Jews? asked the Germans. Hard work would change them from being parasites. Jews were seized and put into forced labor gangs under the direction of the military authorities. To the Jews fell the task of making the streets once more passable and of restoring Warsaw to a habitable city.

The German civilian administration took over from the military in a relatively short time and quickly put into effect its own version of law and order. That did not interfere with the press gangs that roamed the streets and broke into houses looking for Jews to be taken for forced labor.

The German administration, so anxious in other spheres to give a semblance of legality to its actions, did nothing to put a stop to such lawlessness. It cynically suggested that the Jews themselves could solve the problem by volunteering for labor. The Jews had an official body, the Jewish Advisory Council (*Judenrat,* in German), the successor to the former Polish body of the same name, that could provide laborers if it chose.

* * *

2

The Kehillah of Warsaw had differed from other Kehillahs in Poland. Warsaw was the capital, the center of government, of commerce and the arts, where the Jews were sophisticated and for the most part nonreligious. The largest Jewish political party was the Bund, anti-Zionist and anticlerical, socialist and fiercely Jewish-nationalist. For a long time the Bund had taken little interest in the Kehillah, which had been recognized by the new Polish government in 1919 as the guardian of Jewish affairs. The Kehillah had been an elected semiautonomous body with the power to collect taxes from all Jewish citizens and with the responsibility for the maintenance of the Jewish cemetery, for Jewish religious instruction, for the licensing of ritual slaughterers, and for the support of specific Jewish charities. In 1936, when Polish anti-Semitism was in full swing, the Bund altered its tactics. It decided to make use of the Kehillah by transforming it into a secular organization representative of all Jews and then using it as a lever to win concessions from the government. The Bund won a plurality in the communal elections to the Kehillah. The government promptly dissolved the Kehillah as an official body. In its place was set up a council to advise the government on Jewish affairs. Its head, Maurycy Majzel, was named the Commissioner for Jewish Affairs. The members of the council were appointed from various organizations, none of them labor or socialist in orientation, in keeping with the proto-fascist nature of the Polish government. They were drawn from the Veterans' Union, the Craftsmen's Union, the Central Merchants' Association, Agudah Israel (Orthodox), the General Zionist Party, ORT (the American-financed organization for vocational training of Jews), the Retailers' Union, and nonpartisan bourgeois circles.

Majzel fled to the East on the outbreak of the war. During the siege of Warsaw the Zionist parties joined forces with the Merchants' Association and other groups to form a Jewish Public Committee. It was headed by Abraham Gepner, the chairman of the Merchants' Association, a devoted communal leader and a beloved philanthropist. The Jewish Public Committee, with the approval of the mayor, on September 13 took on itself the tasks of safeguarding the goods and property of Jewish businessmen who had left the city, of giving financial aid to needy Jews, and of setting up an emergency hospital in the old Jewish quarter of the city. Despite the danger of moving around in the streets under the rain of bombs and artillery fire, meetings were held almost daily at the former Kehillah building at 26 Grzybowska Street. Adam Czerniakow, a certified engineer, was an active member of the committee.

The Jewish Public Committee was an anomalous body. Although Mayor Starzyński had recognized it as acting in the interests of the Jews, it had no true official status. The committee wanted such status to establish the legality of its trusteeship over Jewish property. On September 22, it sent a letter to Mayor Starzyński, asking that it be attached to the municipal council. Instead, Starzyński the following day announced that the old Jewish Advisory Council with its former members was to represent the Jewish population of Warsaw. Adam Czerniakow was named as "Head of the Jewish Religious Community of Warsaw."

No conflict arose between the Jewish Public Committee and the Jewish Advisory Council. Four days later Warsaw surrendered. The Germans ordered Gepner, the Bundist leader Samuel Zygelboim, the Polish socialist leader Miedzalkowski, and a number of other public figures to report as hostages to ensure that the Poles and Jews of Warsaw maintained order, especially around the soup kitchens. In the absence of its chairman, Gepner, the Jewish Public Committee ceased to function. The Jewish Advisory Council remained as the sole body engaged in providing for the needs of the Jewish community in Warsaw.

3

Adam Czerniakow was born in Warsaw on November 30, 1880, into a moderately well-to-do family. He had a modern education, going through the university courses in the chemistry division of the Warsaw People's Technicum; after that he went to Dresden for advanced studies, finally meeting all the requirements to be an industrial engineer. His school years were apolitical; he took no part in the revolutionary anti-Tsarist or anti-Russian student movements.

During the Tsarist regime, in his late twenties and still apolitical, Czerniakow, because of his interest in education, was active in the "University for All," a semilegal institution founded by the first organizers of the socialist movement in Poland.

Before 1914 he was apparently uninterested in Jewish affairs, but during the German occupation of Warsaw in World War I he became an activist in the Central Union of Jewish Craftsmen and served as its chairman.

From May, 1919, to June, 1921, he worked in the Ministry of Public Works in the newly independent Republic of Poland.

In 1921 the American Joint Distribution Committee (known familiarly as the "Joint"), an organization disbursing funds donated by American Jews for the relief of Jews in other countries, invited him to become the head of the section of rehabilitation and reconstruction of Jewish housing destroyed in the war. Such work by a private philanthropic organization was needed because already the Polish government was disregarding the obligations it had agreed to in the National Minorities Protocol of the Versailles Treaty. In 1922 Czerniakow made a survey for the Joint, in which he made proposals for the establishment of Jewish vocational schools in Poland.

He kept up his activity in the Craftsmen's Union, succeeding for a time in his attempts to unite the various factions. His emphasis was on cooperation and displays of patriotism for the Polish government. He organized public demonstrations with flags and parades to show the ruling officials that the Jewish craftsmen were Poles as well as Jews.

Despite his avowed Polish patriotism, Czerniakow was ambitious, aspiring to be a leader among the Jews. He hoped that his good work for the Joint would work in his favor so that he would be sent to Geneva to the Jewish Agency as the Joint's representative of Polish Jewry. He was disappointed; another got the post. At the same time he lost his position. The Joint's Cooperative Bank, which had financed his department, was dissolved. He got a large sum of money as severance pay, which he promptly invested in a corporation that just as promptly went bankrupt. He then took a post in a semiofficial body known as the Institute for Foreign Commerce. From then on, either out of conviction or out of a desire not to get fired, he drew somewhat closer to the ideas of the Sanacja Party, conservative and ultranationalistic. Czerniakow's position was assimilationist. He felt that Jews, for almost a thousand years part of the Polish people, were full Polish citizens, not to be classified in the same category as Ukrainians or Ruthenians. As Polish citizens they should be willing to give up the special privileges of the National Minorities Protocol (already a dead letter for the most part) and should insist on their full rights as equals of Christian Poles. Assimilationism was hotly debated in the Craftsmen's Union. Its short-lived unity disappeared. The "folk" group began to gain more adherents. Czerniakow became the leader of the opposition to the "folk" group and wrote for the opposition's publication, *The Free Artisans' Voice.* Many of his articles dealing with the life of Jewish craftsmen were reprinted in the general organ, *The Artisans' Newspaper.* In 1924 he wrote an extensive essay for the tenth anniversary bulletin of the organization on the need for apprenticeship training and vocational schools for Jews. He believed in what he wrote: he taught vocational courses in the schools set up by the Kehillah.

The idea of equality through assimilation was popular in all strata of Jewish society, but the Polish regime was not interested in considering Jews as first-class citizens. Beset by economic crisis, the government laid the blame for its difficulties on the Jews. Discriminatory laws against them were introduced into the Sejm (National Assembly) and passed. The *numerus clausus* restricted the number of Jews who would be permitted to enter the universities. The government hoped by this measure to secure the support of the professionals who felt themselves menaced by Jewish doctors, lawyers, and engineers. Then, in 1927, came the laws for the licensing of Jewish craftsmen. Difficult and complicated examinations had to be passed, and despite the fact that doctors and lawyers could practice regardless of their age once they had passed their examinations, craftsmen like carpenters and shoemakers could not work at their trades until they were thirty years old. Czerniakow, to maintain his authority with the craftsmen, was forced to oppose such laws and to carry on a campaign for their repeal. For this he was criticized in the Engineers' Union of Warsaw, of which he was a member. The Engineers' Union was a center of assimilationism; no language other than Polish was permitted to be used in its meetings; Yiddish was out of the question; Russian and German, the tongues in which the engineers had been taught, were also forbidden.

Czerniakow's position on Jewishness was ambiguous. He favored assimilation, yet he permitted his name to be entered on the list of national minority candidates for the Senate, and later as part of the Jewish National Bloc. The latter led to his acceptance by the Jewish Agency Committee in Warsaw as a delegate for the non-Zionists. In 1931 he was elected to the Senate as a member of the Jewish National Bloc but he never took his seat, the Senate, indeed the whole National Assembly, being dissolved before it held its first meeting. At that time he was also elected to the Warsaw Municipal Council as the representative of the craftsmen.

In 1936, after the dissolution of the Kehillah, he was nominated by the government as vice-president of the new Jewish Advisory Council. Here he continued, as did others on the Council, to propound his assimilationist viewpoint. When Majzel, the president of the Council, fled from Warsaw, he automatically became its head, but the Council no longer functioned.

During the siege of Warsaw, Czerniakow, as a patriotic Polish citizen, enlisted in a Civil Guard organization whose purpose was to prevent the looting of bombed buildings. As a Jew, he took his post at 26 Grzybowska Street, at the former Kehillah building. The house at Number 27 was bombed on September 11; three persons were killed and others wounded. The Civil Guard took care of the wounded with the aid of some volunteers. That incident on top of the increasing distress in the Jewish quarter pointed up the need for a specific organization to care for the Jewish population. The same day Czerniakow attended a conference at Gepner's house concerning such an organization.

The formal organization of the Jewish Public Committee took place the next day. Present were Czerniakow, Gepner, Marek Lichtenboim, Moshe Kerner, Apollinaire Maximilian Hartglas, and Professor Abraham Weis. Duties were apportioned among the self-constituted members of the committee. Czerniakow started to work at once. He helped to gather food, to provide temporary shelters, and to set up a 100-bed emergency hospital for the wounded. In addition, every night he reported for guard duty.

He worked with the Jewish Public Committee but he was undoubtedly piqued at not being its head, a post he felt was his by right of his nominal position as head of the Jewish Advisory Council. Shortly before the surrender of Warsaw he was met one afternoon by Hartglas, a former deputy to the Sejm, in the waiting room of Mayor Starzyński. Hartglas was not backward about asking Czerniakow the reason for his presence nor was Czerniakow backward about answering. He said quite frankly that he wanted an official appointment by Starzyński as head of the Jewish community of Warsaw. He knew that the Polish administration would not last once the Germans took over. He knew how the Germans liked law and order; they would probably retain the existing bureaucracy with supervision of its activities.

The very next day Czerniakow proudly displayed to Hartglas a letter signed and sealed by Starzyński confirming his appointment. He had already had cards printed in German: "Senator Engineer Adam Czerniakow, Chairman of the Warsaw Jewish Community." He said that he had had the cards printed in German so that he could use them with the conquerors; the senatorial designation he felt was his by right because at the very last elections to the Sejm his name followed that of Professor Schoor, who was at the bottom of the elected list; Professor Schoor had fled from Poland, thereby automatically elevating Czerniakow to the senatorial seat. Czerniakow said that the Germans were impressed by titles and would respect him more were he a Senator. He looked respectable enough, a typical man of the bourgeoisie, clean-shaven, tall, stout, always in a black suit, restrained and deliberate in his movements and speech.

Czerniakow was a self-deceiver, it appears. Hartglas's story portrays Czerniakow as an opportunist, eager to have honor for honor's sake. Yet Czerniakow wrote in his personal diary, "This is a historic role in a city under siege. I shall try to live up to it."

In the days succeeding the surrender of Warsaw, he indeed tried to fulfill the role of leader. He offered himself to the Germans as a hostage as a pledge of Jewish cooperation in the restoration of order. He evidently believed that the Germans, a cultured people, would not kill hostages. The future was unseen; the past gave precedents for humane treatment; the present demanded that a Jewish leader stand as a true representative of his brothers. But the Germans already had hostages; they neither needed him nor accepted his noble offer. He turned then to his role as chairman of the Council.

4

The new Council met in the building at 26 Grzybowska Street and began to function immediately, taking over the tasks previously performed by the voluntary Jewish Public Committee. It had plenty to do. Warsaw was still in a state of chaos with the intermingled authority of the former Polish municipal administration, German military commanders, and the Gestapo soon to be added to by officials of the SS. On October 7, 1939, the Gestapo took over the civil administration of the city. As Czerniakow had expected, the existing officials were confirmed in their posts, including those of the Jewish Advisory Council.

The Germans were not as polite in the present occupation of Warsaw as they had been in the First World War. Now they had no qualms about the treatment of inferior races like the Poles or subhumans like the Jews. Quickly and efficiently they set about despoliation as a preliminary to extermination.

Czerniakow was summoned to Gestapo headquarters. He was

told that the Germans had no interest in Jews other than to see that the German orders were promptly obeyed. He was directed to see that the Judenrat have at least twenty-four members and an equal number of alternates. Immediate arrangements were to be made for a census of the Jews and for provision of contingents for labor gangs. Workers were needed for the renovation of the Sejm building, for the clearing of rubble, for cleaning of garages and barracks, and for the construction of a new airfield. It was up to the Judenrat to see to it that sufficient men were supplied daily for these needs. The summary seizure of Jews on the streets and in their homes would be halted if the Judenrat did its work well.

Czerniakow told his associates on the Council of its new name and responsibilities. The Judenrat existed only for the convenience of the Germans as an instrument to carry out its directives. Czerniakow, as its head, was personally answerable to the Gestapo. The Judenrat was expressly forbidden to engage in any communal activities with the exception of providing burials. Czerniakow wangled from the Germans permission to resume the social services so desperately needed: the upkeep of the hospital and the provision of cash relief for the destitute. But when he asked for funds from the city treasury to be allotted for those purposes, he was cynically told, "Charge higher burial fees. That will be your main source of income."

Czerniakow immediately went about the organization of the Judenrat. A number of the members of the former Jewish Advisory Council still remained in Warsaw; they automatically became members of the Judenrat. Having been appointed by the reactionary Polish regime, they were (with the exception of the Orthodox and General Zionist representatives) for the most part assimilationists, all from the professional and commercial classes, conservative in viewpoint. To them Czerniakow added others of the same classes. Of necessity he coopted Samuel Zygelboim, the leader of the Bund, the largest proletarian party, because he felt there should be at least one delegate from the working class. Zygelboim's participation in the Judenrat was of short duration;

he made his way to London after a fiery open speech advocating resistance to the Germans. Czerniakow did approach leading Zionists of the left, but they peremptorily refused at this time to take part in what they called collaboration with the Nazi enemy. (Later, less scrupulous because of hunger, many of them became minor officials in the Judenrat offices.) Czerniakow was an excellent executive; he chose those men he thought would be good managers, not mere figureheads. As a result, he was not over-careful as to the effect his appointments made on the Jewish masses. For example, after the ghetto was established, he made Szerynski, a convert to Catholicism and a bitter anti-Semite, the head of the *Ordnungsdienst,* the Jewish police, because Szerynski had been an inspector of police under the Polish government. As a matter of fact, he favored converts and assimilationists who had had little to do with Jewish affairs before the war. Reproached for putting such people in high position, Czerniakow replied, "We are no longer the Jewish community of before the war, but the Jewish part of the capital where all inhabitants enjoy the same rights," or lack of them under German rule, he meant. He also said, "What else can I do when your honest and upright people are incompetent? At least these knaves, as you call them, are industrious and I get good use of them."

Czerniakow called a public meeting, one of the few held by the Judenrat. At one point in his address he said, "I now find myself in a post which I did not assume on my own initiative and of which I cannot divest myself. I am not independent, and I do only what is possible." He was not exactly disingenuous. He had applied for the post, but evidently now he was having second thoughts about its honor and prestige. He implied that he would carry out German orders but would not go out of his way to accommodate himself to them.

The Germans' brand of law and order was consistent with their ideas of racial superiority. Jews, despite Czerniakow's fond idea that they were going to be treated as Jewish Polish citizens, were singled out for special treatment. On October 12, it was decreed that all gold, silver, and other precious metals held by Jews were to be turned over to the Germans; the results of the decree were disappointing to the Germans; the Jews took care to hide their valuables. All bank accounts of Jews were blocked; 250 zlotys could be withdrawn weekly for personal use; larger amounts needed for communal purposes or to pay wages or installments on loans required specific permission from the Gestapo. Evasion took place on a large scale; ethnic Germans, seeing a chance to get rich quickly, cooperated. Jews said they owed large sums to these Volksdeutsche. When the money was withdrawn, they split it fifty-fifty with their newfound friends.

"Legal" expropriation was too slow for the Germans. On October 14, two Gestapo officers appeared at the Judenrat building and demanded the keys to the safe. Czerniakow had the keys; he was sent for, and the safe was opened. It contained, besides the Judenrat's own funds, money deposited by emigrés for safekeeping until they could send for it from their places of refuge, as well as money and jewelry found on the bodies of unidentified Jewish corpses during the siege of Warsaw. About 90,000 zlotys in cash and the jewelry were taken. Czerniakow protested and said he needed the money to pay salaries. The Gestapo officers said curtly, "You'll manage," and left.

Czerniakow tried to pursue his customary existence despite the semi-anarchy that was Warsaw. He went to work daily at his job in the city, and after that to the Judenrat building, with frequent command visits to SS or Gestapo headquarters at any time of the day and night. He found that the Germans thought little of him: he would have to wait for hours in the corridors of their offices; once he was kept overnight and "bothered," as he euphemistically called the beating he was subjected to. The Poles treated him little better: his badge as member of the Civil Guard was ripped from his coat; his co-workers cut him on the street; the management hinted he should resign. Stopped once by German soldiers for a work gang, he had difficulty convincing them that he had special privileges as a liaison officer with the SS for the Jewish community. He said of that occasion, "When I got home, I vomited from fear." He may have felt ashamed of himself for being a physical coward but he continued to try to do his duty as a Jewish leader.

Warsaw's main problem was food. The emergency soup kitchens set up by the Germans supplied some nourishment, and other provisions were brought into the city by peasants from the surrounding areas. Those who had money could buy; the others went hungry. The Germans quickly organized a relief system for the Polish inhabitants of Warsaw but not for the Jews; yet the money for the Polish relief was taken from the Social Security Fund to which the Jews had also contributed. The Judenrat had practically no money. The needs of the hungry Jews were left entirely in the hands of the Joint and the much smaller international agencies (TOZ, CENTOS, ORT) which were not primarily relief agencies. Czerniakow, on behalf of the Judenrat, undertook negotiations to raise loans from various banks where Jews had large accounts; he hoped that the funds would be unblocked or that liens on future taxes would be taken as security for the loans.

The forced labor with its accompanying beatings and indignities was a sore burden for the Jews. Czerniakow proposed to the Germans that he would provide 500 laborers daily. The offer was accepted, but the press gangs still continued to operate.

Czerniakow had to visit the Gestapo headquarters frequently, there to receive orders and decrees for whose execution he was held responsible. The decrees were published in three languages: German, Polish, and Yiddish. One edict followed another, all aimed at the denigration and despoliation of the Jews. Jewish businesses had to display the yellow insignia of the Shield of David; individual Jews had to wear similar armbands. All Jewish schools were closed; Jewish children were not allowed to attend Polish schools. Pensions drawn by retired Jews were abolished. "Trusteeships" under the control of Germans took over large Jewish enterprises.

The census of registered Jews showed 360,000 in Warsaw. On November 5, 1939, the Gestapo informed Czerniakow that a Jewish ghetto was to be set up and its boundaries were outlined; 160,000 Jews from other parts of Warsaw were to be moved into the designated area. The Judenrat was in an uproar over the news. A delegation went to General Neumann, the military commander of Warsaw, and pointed out to him that such a move was not only inhumane and a throwback to the Middle Ages but was also totally unfeasible. A typhoid epidemic was raging in Warsaw. The Jewish hospital and the cemetery lay outside the lines of the proposed ghetto. Such a mass movement of people as was envisioned would endanger the lives of German soldiers as well as of the Polish civilian population. General Neumann, who had not been informed of the Gestapo plan, immediately rescinded the order. The Gestapo chiefs were enraged by the *chutzpah* of the Jews in going over their heads. To ensure that the Gestapo would not go ahead anyway, a delegation headed by Dr. Henryk Szoszkes went to Krakow, the capital of the General-Gouvernment, to see Dr. Hans Frank, the recently appointed governor. He agreed that no ghetto would be set up. The Gestapo, frustrated, ordered that signs be put up around the old Jewish quarter, warning of the danger of infectious disease in the area, particularly typhus fever spread by "lousy Jews."

The prospect of a ghetto had frightened some Jews into voluntarily leaving their apartments in the city to crowd into the old Jewish quarter. Polish landlords and German expropriators forced others out. The Judenrat was besieged with demands for redress. Czerniakow wrote, "If the order for resettlement had not been rescinded, it would have been impossible to withstand the complaints of the Jews."

Of complaints there was no lack. Relief was needed for the hungry and homeless refugees, communal workers were unpaid, the orphan asylum and the hospital needed supplies. Czerniakow had real as well as figurative headaches. "My head explodes . . . I have the problems of the families thrown out of the suburbs, the hospital, the orphan asylum, the displaced lunatics wandering the streets. My head is splitting . . . Headache powders morning and night . . ." He developed insomnia and often spent all night reading. Before his fifty-ninth birthday on November 30, 1939, he wrote in his diary a comment revelatory both of his systematic mode of thought and his ideology: "At one time I made a division of my life into three stages: (1) education and pleasure, (2) occupation, and (3) reconciliation with God and self-appraisal. Fate has drawn a cancellation through my calculations. . . ."

Greater and greater demands were made on the Judenrat by the Jewish community for relief. Large amounts of money were frozen in Jewish bank accounts, but getting even small sums was beset by difficulties. The Polish bank managers were bureaucrats; they wanted security in the form of mortgages on Jewish property outside the old Jewish quarter for any loans they extended, even though hundreds of thousands of zlotys belonging to Jews lay in their vaults. The Germans were arbitrary in their refusal to allow withdrawals. Furthermore, in the middle of November they demanded a "voluntary contribution" of 300,000 zlotys. Of that amount 40,000 zlotys were raised in cash and the rest was offered in the form of credit transfers from foreign funds. The Germans wanted all cash. They ordered six rabbis, six wealthy Jews, and five members of the Judenrat to be held as hostages until the full payment was made. Czerniakow intervened and said he would be personally responsible for the balance if the hostages were released. By means of an emergency collection and with the help of the Joint, the whole sum was raised.

Unfortunately for Czerniakow's reputation among the Jews, a few days previously all the men in the housing complex at 9 Nalewki Street had been arrested on trumped-up charges. Fifty-three of them were shot. The families of the victims cursed Czerniakow and called him a murderer, charging his slowness in raising the "contribution" with causing the deaths.

On December 12, 1939, Higher-SS-and-Police-Leader Krüger, on behalf of the General-Gouvernement signed a decree empowering the Judenrat to organize labor contingents for the use of any German agency that wanted them. The decree provided a way out of the press gangs; order was introduced into the forced labor system. The press gangs grew smaller in number—and the Judenrat had a better source of income than burial fees. The German agency notified the Judenrat how many men it needed; the Judenrat supplied the quota. That was easy now that the Judenrat had the authority to punish all those who disobeyed it. All Jews between the ages of sixteen and sixty-five had to register for work nine days a month; they would receive nothing for their work from the Germans, but the Judenrat would be paid a minimum sum. The Judenrat gave them an additional wage and supported their families after a fashion. All were equal. But not quite. The Judenrat derived an income from the labor quotas because exemptions could be purchased by the payment of 60 zlotys a month. By July, 1940, as many as 10,000 men daily were supplied by the Judenrat—and the payment for exemptions figured heavily in its budget.

Additional income was derived from the charges the disinfection department made for its services. Typhus fever was on the increase, not surprising in view of the prevalence of lice in the crowded living quarters. Czerniakow himself underwent the procedure of delousing, marveling at the devotion of the hospital personnel who took such fearful chances of getting typhus fever. He wrote in his diary, excusing himself for getting antityphus fever vaccine injections, "I am needed for my fellow-men, more than for myself."

With every increase of income came more demands for money. Jews who were caught without the yellow patch were not released until the community paid 100 zlotys per person. A Volksdeutsche said he had been beaten by a gang of Jews; the community was fined 100,000 zlotys. The Polish Tax Office demanded 500,000 zlotys due from Jews for taxes dating as far back as 1930. Czerniakow, desperate, asked for permission to go to neutral Holland to raise money for the Jews. Permission was refused on the ground that as head of the Jewish community he was indispensable.

He was discharged from his job. "God knows on what I'll live," he wrote, "since I don't want to take anything from the community and actually I keep laying out money for my expenses there."

He fought in vain to get rehired, but he did succeed in getting severance pay in the form of three months' salary to be paid in monthly installments over a year.

In spite of the work force supplied by the Judenrat, occasional arbitrary seizures of Jews on the streets still took place. Beatings of Jews and looting of Jewish stores were daily occurrences. Czerniakow went repeatedly to the Gestapo to intervene for arrested individuals. He felt his position was intolerable. Finally he went to Brandt, the SS leader, and asked to be released from his post as chairman of the Judenrat because he could not carry out his duties under such abnormal conditions. Brandt said no.

The rationing regulations instituted by the Germans applied only to Poles. Jews had to fend for themselves on the free market. Sellers of food steadily raised prices. Actual hunger began to be part of Jewish life. The winter was cold. Stores with special permits sold briquettes and coal at a price theoretically fixed by the Germans, but free enterprise actually set the price. Coal was sold for amounts "passed under the table." As a result only wealthy Jews could afford to buy coal. The majority of their "race comrades" shivered and froze.

On January 21, 1940, a decree was issued ordering the registration of Jewish property of all kinds. The Jews saw in the decree a preliminary to confiscation. Immediately there began wild trading and deals in the ranks of the upper Jewish bourgeoisie. Merchandise was hidden away; stores were left half-empty; trustworthy Poles became overnight the titular owners of businesses, but not for long because the German courts soon ruled that such transfers of ownership made shortly before or after the invasion of Poland were invalid. Large stocks of goods were sold cheaply and the proceeds of the sales promptly invested in such easily hidable or transportable objects as diamonds, specie, and stamps. Within six months 75 percent of Jewish industrial and commercial enterprises were sold or liquidated. Hungry and cold, the lower classes grinned at the hysteria of their former bosses.

But the Germans made no class distinctions when it came to Jews. The religious Jews, mainly poor refugees from the provinces, were forbidden to hold congregational worship, and "for humane reasons" ritual slaughter was likewise prohibited. Craftsmen were ordered to (but for the most part did not) turn in the tools of their trade. Jews were forbidden to engage in various occupations, including printing and carting. More and more of the small traders, the little merchants, the artisans, and the skilled mechanics were forced into the ranks of the unemployed and had to be supported by the Judenrat and the Joint.

The Joint and other international agencies got permission for some Jews to emigrate to Palestine. The Germans lost nothing by the deal. They confiscated all the property of the emigrés, and each emigré was expected to pay 600 zlotys to the Judenrat for a fund earmarked for expenses "for the future resettlement of the Jews after the war." Czerniakow attacked those Jews who left without paying the 600 zlotys because they were abandoning the Jewish community. He refused to let his name be entered on the list of emigrés; he felt his duty lay in Warsaw. He was openly contemptuous of Hartglas and Kerner, his old comrades of the Jewish Public Committee, when they bade him good-bye. He sneered at Kerner's promise to raise money for the Warsaw Jews once he was out of Nazi hands.

The Joint received large sums of money from the United States, but the Jews soon bitterly realized that the American dollars were insufficient for their needs. The Germans demanded that the dollars be exchanged for zlotys at the official rate, which was much lower than the market rate. In effect, the 80 percent difference in the money realized went to the Germans. Furthermore, the offices of the Joint were strained to bursting with applicants for relief, not only from Warsaw but also from all over occupied Poland. "Those who are nearest the spoon get the first lick," openly lamented the poor Jews. "If you don't have pull, don't even bother to go to the Joint."

Class demarcations increased. Rich Jews not only could afford to pay for exemptions from the forced labor but could buy substitutes to go in their names, thus enabling them to evade the Judenrat tax. Imprisonment (for illegal trading, for not wearing the Jewish badge, for any of a dozen offenses) could be avoided by the payment of a fine plus a bribe, the cost of which rose from 2,000 to 5,000 zlotys in a few months. In line with the principle of "all are equal," the Judenrat issued ration cards. They were valid for only a limited amount of bread, yet Jewish bakeries displayed and sold fancy rolls, cakes, and pastries. Czerniakow, supported by his Judenrat, could not conceive of interfering with free enterprise; he felt himself helpless under the workings of Adam Smith's Invisible Hand.

Czerniakow, too, felt the pinch of beginning impoverishment. He was living on his capital. His position as Chairman was unpaid. His wife complained to him about the black market and the indignities she suffered while standing in line for food. He became resentful of the curses piled on his head. "The Jews need a scapegoat, and I'm it," he wrote. On one occasion, in the Judenrat building, he lost his temper and called a woman a whore for spreading the story that he was getting a good salary while the clerks and the workers got a mere pittance, and that only after long delays.

Suddenly the power of the Judenrat over the Jews was increased. The Germans again notified Czerniakow that he was fully and personally responsible for carrying out their orders for the "members of the Jewish race." His authority to levy taxes was enlarged. The *Kultussteuer* (the tax formerly levied for support of Kehillah activities) was reinstated. To it was added the right to charge for the issuance of the monthly ration cards, a residence tax, an income tax on the wealthy and on the "trustees" of former Jewish enterprises (a tax that existed only on paper because it was never paid), a handling charge of 0.2 percent when the Judenrat acted as intermediary for the withdrawal from blocked accounts of funds needed by individuals in their businesses, and a variety of other indirect taxes. About the same time, well-secured loans were made to the Judenrat by several banks. Out of the increased income the Judenrat had to pay city taxes levied by the municipal administration and, more important, charges made by the Germans for various "expenses." The Germans actually took 40 percent of the income during the first six months of 1940. One of the "expenses" was in connection with a wall that was to be built. For that purpose came a German demand for more laborers. The wall was to be constructed across certain designated streets without trolley lines.

Rumors about a ghetto had come and gone since the rescinding of the November, 1939, decree. The signs "DANGER! INFECTIOUS DISEASE!" posted at the outskirts of the old Jewish quarter had caused fear of a closed ghetto, but months had passed since the signs were up and nothing had happened. The fear gradually subsided. Every time some streets in Warsaw were made *Judenrein,* the same fears recurred, only to go away when Jews were permitted to move elsewhere in the city. The wall revived all the fears, especially since it was to be made of brick with only a limited number of gates. The Germans told Czerniakow that the wall was to be for the protection of the Jews from anti-Semitic attacks by Poles, which indeed had greatly increased since the introduction of the yellow badge. Czerniakow had no faith in the German protestations of concern for the safety of the Jews. He had been told cold-bloodedly only a few days previously that Jews had been shot for breaking laws and more would be shot.

Some optimists saw in the wall the beginning of Hitler's end. The wall, the rumor spread, was to limit street actions in the event of a revolt by the Poles. Talk of a closed ghetto, such as already existed in Lodz, was revived but was ridiculed. "Even the Germans wouldn't revert to such a medieval idea in the heart of civilized Europe! . . . Beasts, yes! Stupid, no! The Nazis wouldn't break up the commercial life of a big city for a propaganda idea. . . . Besides, why do we need a wall for a ghetto? We're practically in a ghetto already!"

Indeed, most of the Jews were. The old Jewish quarter of Warsaw was crowded with refugees and with Jews whose apartments had been requisitioned by the Germans. Families had been forced to live with relatives and friends back in the poor neighborhoods from which they had risen. In addition, the Jewish patch was an ever-present incitement to anti-Semitic Poles and German soldiers. Jews felt safer and more comfortable among their fellow-sufferers. They cracked bitter jokes. "Nalewki Street [in the Jewish section] is like Hollywood. Why? Because there are so many stars to be seen!" Over two thirds of the Jews of Warsaw were crowded into a more or less voluntary ghetto.

On May 3, 1940, Hendl, a Jew on good terms with the Gestapo, told Czerniakow that a closed ghetto was being contemplated. Czerniakow merely noted the information in his diary along with the news that the Germans wanted more laborers, a demand that would mean a greater income for the Judenrat. He also noted on June 4 that the Judenrat treasury had a good day: "18,000 zlotys came in from funeral permits." Not until June 29 did he remark that he was going to check on the validity of the rumors about a ghetto.

On July 1 he heard from the Germans that all the Jews would be evacuated to Madagascar, hence no ghetto was in the offing. On July 5 he received official word from Krakow that Warsaw would have no ghetto. On July 16 he noted, "There will definitely be no ghetto."

The Germans were not taking Czerniakow into their confidence. On August 11 an order came that Jews were to reside within the borders of the Jewish Residential District. And in September, 1940, came the notice that the Jewish quarter was to be closed off from the rest of the city in order to quarantine the "lousy Jews" who spread typhus fever and other epidemic diseases. Special permission was needed to go out of or come into the Quarantine Area.

The optimism of the Jews that they would survive Hitlerian oppression, as they had that of the Poles and the Tsars, began to fade as hunger spread throughout the area. The markets in the rest of the city were cut off by the decree. The regulations against movement across the boundaries were evaded. Poles and Jews organized widespread smuggling of food into the area. The provisions brought in were paid for in cash or by barter in merchandise to be sold in "Aryan" Warsaw (knitwear, toys, linens, socks, etc.). Of course, only the wealthy could afford to buy the food at the smugglers' prices. The Joint, its funds almost exhausted, was now of little help to the poor. The Judenrat became the focus of the demands for relief.

Czerniakow did try to alleviate the distress. He went to Leist, the German City Governor. Leist received him politely and explained that the Jewish question was a special one and that he could do nothing without orders from above. Czerniakow went to the new Polish mayor of Warsaw, Julian Kulski. Kulski, in a self-justifying statement after the war, said of these meetings on the relief of the Jews, "Czerniakow understood very well the inability of the city administration to contribute to the needs of the Jewish segment of the population; therefore he never presented any unreasonable demands to the municipality. . . ." Czerniakow may not have. He prided himself on being a reasonable man; he felt that it would be a wrong tactic to press the rights of Jews as Polish citizens at that time. He got sympathy from Kulski, nothing more. Yet—at that very moment Kulski knew very well about the forty million zlotys concealed from the Germans, money taken from the national funds and hidden when the last Polish government fled from the city. Not two groszy were given to Czerniakow, not even covertly!

The only concession Czerniakow got from the Gestapo in his dealings with it was permission to assess the Jews for the opening of schools later in the autumn. The school tax was impossible to collect. The Judenrat had no right to impose sanctions for non-payment, no more than it had for failure to pay taxes for the upkeep of the Jewish hospital. Unlike Rumkowski, Czerniakow did not take on himself nor did he ask the Germans for the right to imprison or fine those delinquent in the support of communal institutions.

The miseries of the Quarantine Area were compounded by the ukase of October 16, 1940, when all subterfuge was dropped and a ghetto proclaimed. Jews living outside the ghetto (about 140,000) were to move into it and all Christians in it (about

80,000) were to move out. Jews had until October 31 to move voluntarily; force would be used after that date. The exact boundaries of the Jewish Residential District—it was forbidden to call it a ghetto—were not defined at the time of the decree. Debates with the Germans about what streets were to be included in the district continued right up to the very day of its final closure. Czerniakow himself did not know which streets were to be Jewish and which "Aryan." He gave up his apartment for one on a street within the area and then had to scrounge around for another when that street was cut off from the ghetto.

Within two weeks, more than 360,000 Jews were squeezed into an area of a hundred square city blocks. The ghetto was irregularly shaped and was further divided into a Small and Large Ghetto connected by a pedestrian bridge that crossed an "Aryan" thoroughfare.

5

Czerniakow was particularly chagrined at the proclamation of the edict. He had confidently told his associates in the Judenrat that quarantine was quarantine, that no ghetto was to be established. He had publicly announced on October 15, the day before the decree, that he had been assured by the General-Gouvernement in Krakow that Warsaw would have no ghetto. But, ever resilient, he accepted the decree and started to busy himself with its administration. He set up a Housing Office to ensure that all who moved in would have shelter. He recruited a thousand young men for an Ordnungsdienst, a service to keep order and to direct traffic. He carried on negotiations with Mayor Kulski to have the city continue its Provisioning Office outside the ghetto to forestall merchants from taking advantage of the Jews' isolation.

Not one of the three projects were of any help. Wealthy Jews from "Aryan" Warsaw paid Housing Department officials to get them good apartments. Poles living in the Jewish Residential District refused to give up their apartments without key money. The managers of the housing complexes (all built around a central courtyard) demanded three months' rent in advance, a practice previously unheard of in Warsaw. In addition, rents rose to as much as five times the pre-ghetto rate. Housing Office officials, their palms well greased, blinked at violations of their regulations. The boundaries of the ghetto shifted as German and Polish industrialists succeeded in getting their factories excluded, as Poles succeeded in keeping some streets for themselves, as parks were exluded, as the Germans were bribed by Jews to include some streets with very modern housing. Moving was accompanied by disorder and despoliation. Truckmen stole loads of furniture or informed the Gestapo that valuables were being brought into the ghetto in violation of German orders. Poles demanded extra payment for immovables (stoves, chandeliers, built-in wardrobes) in their apartments; Jews were not compensated for leaving behind such immovables.

The Jewish Ordnungsdienst, the O.D., imitated the corrupt Polish police they were so familiar with. They settled arguments over apartments by favoring the contestant who forked over the most money. They searched porters carrying sacks and lifted for themselves what they chose. They supervised unloadings and saw that nothing was stolen—for a generous tip. The masses had hoped that a Jewish policeman would be more sympathetic to his fellow-Jews than a Polish policeman. On the contrary, he lorded it over them, taking advantage of his knowledge of their customary ways so that he was not so easily deceived as his Polish counterparts. Sons of the bourgeoisie, for the most part assimilated, they looked down on the workers and the petty traders. And the latter, in turn, grew to hate the Jewish police and the Judenrat for building such a force.

Czerniakow feared that the Jewish Residential District would eventually become a tightly closed ghetto like the one in Lodz. In Warsaw movement was still relatively free in and out of the ghetto, but he felt that freedom was to be short-lived. The Germans, when he discussed with them the financial problems he was having, suggested that he confiscate and sell the stores of merchandise the Jews had in the ghetto. On Czerniakow's objection to such an outrageous proposal, the Germans told him he could have an additional source of income through a tax he could levy on those entering or leaving the ghetto on business. Czerniakow also knew that if the ghetto was closed, the Germans would be the sole providers of food for its inhabitants (at the incredibly low level of less than 800 calories a day per person) and would make the Jews pay dearly for that food. He tried to manipulate and maneuver to prevent such a situation. Dr. Fischer, the governor of the Warsaw district, would brook no changes in the method of provisioning, gloating that "the Jews will disappear because of hunger and need, and nothing will remain of the Jewish question but a cemetery."

When the ghetto was finally closed on November 15, 1940, the only legal place of exchange was the Umschlagsplatz, where provisions could be bought by the Judenrat and private individuals and where goods manufactured in the ghetto were to be sent out to be sold at fixed prices in "Aryan" Warsaw or to the German army. The *Transferstelle* would be the agency for transmitting orders to the ghetto industries. Czerniakow was directed to supply good furniture for twenty rooms at the Transfer Office—and to "contribute" 6,000 zlotys for the Winter Olympic Games.

6

Technically, by the terms of his appointment by the Germans, Czerniakow was the dictator over the ghetto. He did not see himself in that role, however, but rather as the chief executive of a corporation with the Judenrat members as his board of directors, an unusual type of corporation with a double set of shareholders to whom he was responsible—the German overlords and the Jewish community. He felt German orders came first. If they were not carried through, the Germans had in their hands effective weapons to enforce their execution directly without the intervention of the Judenrat—starvation, revival of the press gangs, outright death. His board of directors agreed with him. The Judenrat would do what it could to restore Jewish communal life, but the maintenance of Jewish life itself was paramount.

Czerniakow was not given a free hand in the appointment of his administrators. Many times Jews came with letters of recommendation from German higher-ups or had German officials intervene for them to get soft jobs. He protested against such pressure, saying, "Out of a sense of responsibility I would not like to be made to select people I don't know." He resisted, for example, the polite but urgent request of Lieutenant-Colonel von Kamlah to give a woman a monopoly of the ghetto bakeries; he was forced, however, to give her sons jobs in the post office.

In contrast to Rumkowski, Czerniakow did not throw his weight around. "The Eldest of the Jews of Litzmannstadt" gloried in his title and presumed on it; the Chairman of the Warsaw Judenrat was fully conscious of the little worth of his title. Czerniakow's policy was one of bending to the regime. He would scrupulously carry out its orders, but he would not go out of his way to cooperate with it. He had a strong sense of responsibility to the Jews he felt he represented; he tried to help them within the limits of his office. His view of those limits was determined by his education and background. He was a liberal, a believer in free enterprise, a typical businessman. He conducted himself as a corporate executive. "It is not easy to visit him," wrote a diarist. "One has to pass a number of receptionists at grilled windows and secretaries in various offices. Often one has to wait for three weeks before getting to see the Chairman; in the meantime the desired interview loses its meaning and the would-be petitioner gives up his turn."

Czerniakow, like Rumkowski, intervened with German authorities about mistreatment of the Jews but, unlike Rumkowski, on completely different grounds. Rumkowski fancied himself a Court Jew responsible to his coreligionists as an intercessor; Czerniakow felt that administration of the Jewish community was hindered by arbitrary beatings and jailings, and as an executive he had to protest against such unbusinesslike dealings as blackmail, confiscation of apartments, and seizure of communal monies. He did exert himself, however, to the point of being told he was a nuisance when he asked for the release of prisoners arrested on various charges.

Czerniakow had been correct in his estimate of what would happen once the ghetto was closed. Food prices on the free market rose to staggering heights and fewer people could buy the extras needed to supplement the starvation ration. Workers cut off from their jobs in "Aryan" Warsaw, retailers and small merchants, professionals, as their cash was exhausted, first peddled off their belongings, then became street-singers or open beggars.

Smuggling now became a big business, fraught with danger but paying well. The ghetto wall was not impermeable: passageways were made through it, under it, and over it. The cemetery was used as the smugglers' exchange place to bring food in and to send goods out to be sold on the free market in the rest of the city. New manufactories sprang up overnight. Shops for making knitwear, shoes, artificial candy and jelly, leather goods and other consumer items used materials smuggled into the ghetto; sales of the finished products were arranged for by telephone and the smugglers took care of the exportation. Jews were licensed to buy scrap materials, paper, and junk of all descriptions to be processed and then sold to the Wehrmacht; much of the material was diverted into other channels for private production, and the finished goods smuggled out to be sold in the city, often to German businessmen. The smugglers became a new elite but, coming from the lower classes as they did, were not hated by the people but were rather honored for their part in alleviating the distress of starvation.

The *platzovniks* were another group that brought food illegally into the ghetto. The *platzovniks* (about 8,000 originally, but their number decreased rapidly) were Jewish labor battalions that left the ghetto daily to work under supervision of Jewish foremen for German agencies. They thus had the opportunity to buy bread and other victuals outside the ghetto for themselves and their families. For that reason, as the hunger in the ghetto increased, workers gave bribes to get into the heavy labor battalions they had previously shunned.

Czerniakow, unlike Rumkowski, winked at the smuggling, so essential to circumvent the German plan of starving out the Jews. His job, he reasoned, was to publish the decrees with their threats of punishment for violators. Enforcement of the decrees would be up to the Germans.

Jewish nationalists saw in the closed ghetto the return of cultural autonomy because now that the Poles and Germans were gone, administration was entirely in the hands of the Judenrat. Indeed, administrative autonomy was quickly established. Czerniakow, the efficient executive, with the aid of his subordinates launched what the nationalists fondly called a "Jewish state." Czerniakow had no such illusions. What they called state offices, he called management, a convenient method of combining the performance of German mandates with the need to enrich the wretched Jewish life in the ghetto. For example, the Germans ordered the cleaning up of bombed-out areas; on Czerniakow's instructions, seven of the areas had playground equipment set up in them for children of kindergarten age.

The Judenrat's slogan was "All are equal!" Actually it should have been "Laissez-faire." Taxes were indeed equal, the same for the rich as for the poor. There was a monthly poll tax, a tax on bread cards, a tax for epidemic control (disinfection squads, etc.), a tax for the police, and a tax for the collection of garbage. In addition, forty-nine other taxes were levied from time to time for special purposes; some of these taxes became permanent, as, for example, the 40 percent tax on prescriptions, the tax being turned over to the general Judenrat treasury. Fees were charged for various reasons: five zlotys for a pass to leave the ghetto for professional purposes (doctors, lawyers, businessmen with German "trustees"), varying amounts for permits to open a store, a factory, a coffee house. Ten percent of the rents collected was allocated to the general treasury of the Judenrat.

Taxes were needed if communal institutions like the hospital were to be maintained. They were needed to pay for the food supplied to those on welfare and to the refugees and deportees who swelled the ranks of the unemployed. But "All are equal!" went against the grain of the helpless poor, of the humanitarians, and of the socialist workers.

They were further enraged when they saw the effects of laissez-faire capitalism. Stores that sold the rationed foods "ran out of them" quickly; for an additional amount under the table the food suddenly appeared. Judenrat officials used their posts to make fortunes; they held several positions at once—Marek Lichtenboim, for instance, drew a salary of 60,000 zlotys a month. Officials took graft in the issuing of permits to open workshops or else became silent partners in the businesses. Nepotism flourished; the administrators needed civil servants—who better than their families and friends? Nightclubs and fancy restaurants opened, serving fine food and liquor, while the death toll from starvation mounted, especially in the refugee centers. The disinfection squads could be paid off not to bother the inhabitants of an apartment. The post office demanded payment for the delivery of mail. A department for Jewish culture under the direction of Dr. Alfred Nossig (a man under the direct protection of high German officials) existed only on paper, but it nevertheless asked that fees be paid for permits to hold parties. The illegal underground organizations carried on their cultural affairs without support from the Judenrat and ignored the demand for fees.

Corruption was endemic in the police force, which eventually comprised 2,000 men. The police wore boots and special hats with stars indicating their rank, and carried batons which they unhesitatingly used to impress the hapless Jews with their power. Servile to the Germans, they were arrogant to the ordinary wearers of the yellow patch. In contrast to Lodz, the underworld contributed only a few members to the police force. Most of the O.D. men were intellectuals and professionals, men who sought cushy jobs at which they could make money. They took bribes, they extorted cash for keeping their eyes and ears closed to smugglers and speculators, they acted as go-betweens (for a commission) for the wealthy and Judenrat agencies. Szerynski, the police chief, finally overreached himself. He was caught by the Germans when he tried to arrange for the sale of confiscated furs to people on the "Aryan" side. He was succeeded by Jacob Leikin, a former officer in the Polish army, a man even more corrupt and cynical than Szerynski had been.

The Germans proposed to Czerniakow the setting up of a system of "national socialism" such as Rumkowski had organized in Lodz, which to them was the model of what a ghetto should be. Czerniakow emphatically refused to have anything to do with such a scheme, much less have special ghetto currency. Here he followed his bent toward conservatism. He was an Adam Smith economist—communism in any form was distasteful to him; he was an assimilationist—anything that would separate the Jews from their Polish fellow-citizens was equally distasteful. One form of planned economy he had to submit to: every week he had to give the Germans his estimate of the amount of food needed and the quantity and type of raw material necessary for production.

Czerniakow was confident that Jewish Warsaw would survive the war were it meanwhile to accommodate itself to the German occupation. His immediate task was to stabilize life in the ghetto so that no disturbances would annoy the Germans. For that he had to have food for the people. At the beginning of 1941 there were 378,979 legally registered Jews in the ghetto, with about another 50,000 illegals. To these were added in February another 72,000 deported from the provinces. Of the total of half a million, only 127,000 were men; the rest were women, youths, and children. Relief was needed at once for the poor and the sick. A small loan was obtained from German banks on the security of the blocked Jewish accounts. New taxes were levied—and new resistance to them arose. An anonymous poster appeared on the Umschlagsplatz: "The first man who pays the Judenrat a single zloty for an anti-typhus inoculation gets a dagger in his belly."

In March of 1941 the Germans applied their racist laws to "Aryan" Warsaw. Another element was added to the ghetto. Jews converted to Catholicism and Catholics whose parents or grandparents had been Jews were pushed inside the walls. Priests wearing the Shield of David celebrated Masses in a church in the ghetto. A Catholic school for the children of converts was set up. Important leaders of prewar Polish society, many of them avowed anti-Semites, found themselves in the company of the abhorred Jews. Noted intellectuals, among them the ardent Catholic Professor Ludwik Hirszfeld, once nominated for the Nobel Prize, were forced to find new occupations in the ghetto. Czerniakow fawned on the converts, gave them preferential treatment in housing, and made them part of his administration. Dr. Joseph Stein, for example, was made head of the hospital. The converts were not as badly off as the Jews when it came to food because Caritas, the Polish Catholic relief organization, sent in food to be distributed among them. Czerniakow's commiserating attitude toward the converts aroused anger in the Jews. One diarist wrote, "I cannot sympathize with their tribulations. One fate for all. I don't doubt that Czerniakow's heart bleeds for them, but destiny has made him a leader in Israel and it doesn't behoove him to spread his wings over apostates and the sons of apostates." In reply to the criticisms directed against him, Czerniakow said, "I cannot approach the problem from a Jewish standpoint but as one affecting the general government of the ghetto. The ghetto is not a Jewish state but a residential area where all must be given equal treatment."

Some were more equal than others. The converts were treated well, but the deportees from the provinces had to pay the Judenrat a special registration fee and extra fees for every parcel of baggage they brought in.

The Jewish intelligentsia expected Czerniakow, as head of the Jewish community, to draw closer to specifically Jewish culture as opposed to Polish culture. That was not the case. He wanted education for the children but not Jewish education. Illustrative was his response to a committee from Ikor (the Jewish Cultural Organization) who came to ask that Yiddish be the obligatory language of the ghetto. Czerniakow laughed and said, "No. Half the members of the Judenrat can't speak or write Yiddish."

Czerniakow did, however, proclaim Saturday as the official day of rest. Cynics pointed to the proclamation as another source of revenue for the Judenrat, not as a concession to the religious feelings of some Jews: by payment of a special tax, beauty parlors, photographers' studios, and other luxury services were permitted to operate.

An unexpected blow came to the upper classes in April, 1941. Sienna Street, where the most modern houses were situated, was cut in half and the Jews living there were forced to seek new accommodations. They had already paid out four kilograms of gold to avert such a disaster only a few weeks before.

A worse blow came to the poor in the same month. The labor battalions working outside the ghetto were discontinued, and with their cessation went a source of smuggled food.

Famine mounted rapidly. Emaciated corpses began to be found on the streets. Deaths from starvation rose to such an extent that the doctors in the hospital discussed plans for scientific research on the wealth of material available. Refugees from Vilna wrote home: "If you can survive in Vilna, don't leave the place . . . My parents and I are starving. Don't come because there is nothing to eat here." Children were deserted in the street in the hope that a kindhearted passerby would take them in. Petty thievery increased. "Snatching," the grabbing of food from a shopper's hands, became a common practice. The Joint was allowed to open an office in the ghetto, but its funds were too limited to have much effect on the famine. The Judenrat said it was doing all it could.

The ghetto masses did not believe that, although one commentator said, "If the Jews of Warsaw who are able to pay had obeyed Czerniakow and willingly turned over the monthly per capita tax, the hunger would be less." The wealthy Jews indeed were neither dependent on nor afraid of the "Jewish government." They evaded taxes by all sorts of subterfuges and quarreled with the tax collectors. The starving people hated the Judenrat for its power over them and its powerlessness before the rich. The populace was suspicious of anything that smacked of officialdom.

When Toporol (an idealistic organization that tried to grow vegetables in windowboxes and vacant lots) called a meeting, the first question from the floor was, "What's your connection with the Judenrat?"

Czerniakow put on a show of piety and tried to placate one group of Jews. Meshulam Kaminer, an Orthodox functionary in charge of selling grave plots, died of typhus. At his funeral, Czerniakow said (in Polish), "Who, of all people, can know better than you what is going on in the Jewish quarter? The starvation, the sickness, the hundreds of dead? You yourself fell victim to those circumstances. We are certain that you, with your deep religious convictions, your abundance of goodwill, will go straight to the Throne of Heaven. Tell Them of our orphans and our widows. We are helpless and we cannot go on much longer. Ask for help for us now, or it may be too late. We are quite sure that your tragic story and your intervention on our behalf will help us." He asked Joseph Szczeransky, a member of Mizrachi (an Orthodox group) to assume Kaminer's post, but Szczeransky said he would rather starve than be a part of the Judenrat bureaucracy. Czerniakow then appointed Hurwitch, a former industrialist who had never taken part in Jewish activities in the past, to the post.

Dr. Ringelblum noted: "The Judenrat has adopted the Tsarist slogan—shut up, don't argue. No discussion and no questions are permitted at its meetings. Czerniakow is like an idol—his word is law." A year before, he had written, "Czerniakow is considered a martyr by many, a man who is simply doing his duty, but others said he was taking on the smell of the Gestapo."

Czerniakow may have appeared like a mighty man to the Jews, but he was not so to the Germans. They arrested him in April of 1941 on suspicion of being involved in shady deals inimical to German interests. His release was obtained only after the Judenrat paid 20,000 zlotys as ransom.

Epidemics swept the ghetto, but the greatest epidemic remained starvation. The Judenrat began to distribute free watery oatmeal gruel to supplement the official ration. New businesses of all sorts opened, and Jews flocked to the workshops so that they could earn a few zlotys more to buy food on the free market. That food, of course, was very expensive. It had been smuggled into the ghetto, and for endangering their lives the smugglers had to be well paid. Small children crawled through openings in the walls to beg for food in "Aryan" Warsaw. Many Poles refused to believe that famine existed on the other side of the wall. A priest in the city told Czerniakow that Jewish children were such skilled beggars that their starving acts appeared real. The number of naked emaciated bodies covered with paper lying in the streets increased; the families of the dead had no money with which to pay for burials. Pinkert, the undertaker, had carts go around picking up the bodies for mass burials in unmarked graves. Dead children were hidden so that their ration cards could be used for the living members of the family.

Most Jews could not afford to buy food, not even for the miserable ration allowed to them. It was estimated that to avoid dying of hunger a family of four needed 1,120 zlotys a month as a minimum over and above the legal ration, which cost 300 zlotys. Sixty percent of the ghetto population depended for sustenance on the ration alone or on the community soup kitchens. There the soup was made from oats, with each portion, given out only once a day, providing only 170 to 200 calories.

With the increasing starvation came increasing moral pollution because the pangs of hunger began to strike at the lower ranks of the bureaucracy. The Gestapo still had a quota for forced labor for its needs inside the ghetto; the Jewish police now filled the quota by its own press gangs, but the police could be bought off for cash. The sons of the rich bribed physicians to give them certificates that they were unfit for work; their fathers paid monthly ransoms to Judenrat officials for exemptions. The police charged tenants of apartments with violations of the blackout regulations; money made them forget the charges. And yet Czerniakow saw in the police a force for law and order and justice. He noted with satisfaction the sight of a policeman giving food to a starving man: "Such a thing would not have been done in any other nation."

In appreciation of their efforts, he gave the police, at a time when the hospital had no money with which to buy food, 100,000 zlotys in full payment of their wages.

Every department of the Judenrat was as corrupt as the police. With the first cold spell, the Housing Commission began distributing coal and briquettes—to their families and friends. The Germans abolished the Small Ghetto and its inhabitants were crowded into the Large Ghetto; the Housing Office arranged for living quarters for zlotys passed in a handshake. For show, the Housing Office did, however, put aside 27,000 zlotys to pay part of the expenses for moving the poor. And the Judenrat covered the expense by a special tax on the bread coupons—equal for all, rich and poor alike—60 groszy per kilogram of bread.

In November, 1941, a Children's Month was declared. Czerniakow himself stood with other members of the Judenrat at street corners, shaking a collection can and affixing paper flowers to the lapels of donors. For the first time, sanctions were imposed for nonpayment of the special tax for the children. The rich were threatened with having lice-ridden refugees billeted in their apartments or with having their sons listed for work camps. At the conclusion of the drive, Czerniakow was praised in a public meeting of the Judenrat as "the First Citizen of the Jewish Quarter." Dr. Ringelblum said on this occasion, "To crown such an incompetent as Czerniakow publicly requires great courage and subservience."

Czerniakow certainly did nothing to enhance his public image. He asked the Germans for permission for private entrepreneurs to open stores to sell tobacco and liquor while thousands had no bread to eat. He kept a dog which had to be fed, while on the steps of the Judenrat building lay children dying from hunger.

He was not altogether heartless, however. He made an inspection of the "points," the quarters for refugees, and was horrified at the sights he saw. "I was glad," he wrote, "to get out into the fresh air to revive myself mentally and physically after the foulness of those places." He gave an order, one of the few he gave on his own initiative, for all the members of the Judenrat to make systematic inspections of the "points" in order to correct the miserable conditions of the refugees.

To the ever-present threat of death from starvation was added another threat. The Polish scout, Henyek, and various Zionist messengers came from Vilna with the dreadful news of the massacre of 30,000 Jews. Some believed the tales of mass executions; some did not. Czerniakow was one of those who did not.

The German noose tightened. More tribute was demanded—in legal form for a change; the ghetto administration was ordered to pay for all gas and electricity bills owed long before the establishment of the ghetto. Indiscriminate beatings by Germans of passersby in the streets became commonplace. Arbitrary confiscations of furniture occurred. The death penalty was ordered for anyone leaving the ghetto without permission. Auerswald, the German commissioner for the ghetto, insisted that the Jews carry out the death sentence on the two men and six women arrested on that charge after the promulgation of the decree, but Czerniakow refused to do so. The Polish police executed the eight. In August, 1941, no correspondence in Hebrew or Yiddish was permitted. In December no food parcels from abroad were allowed to come into the ghetto. The Joint, as an American agency, ceased its operations after Pearl Harbor. All mail deliveries stopped after December 17, 1941.

Czerniakow asked Auerswald whether the new rules presaged the evacuation of the Jews from Warsaw. Auerswald said no such evacuation was contemplated. Czerniakow evidently had doubts about the honesty of the reply because he told Auerswald that if such a forced migration was in store, the Jews would respond better to psychologic measures rather than to fear and terror. The unasked-for advice reflected both Czerniakow's willing bending to German orders and his desire to protect the Jews.

Auerswald no longer treated Czerniakow with the same official correctness as in the past. Sarcasm and insults were part of every interview. Yet Czerniakow kept his temper and remained the gentleman, answering back without fear. Once when Auerswald told him, "Speed up your talk," he replied, "I am not a chatterbox. You give us no concessions. At least give me the concession to talk." His attitude did not impress the Germans. To his argument that there was no room in the Large Ghetto for the inhabitants of the Small Ghetto, he was told, "You're ingenious. You'll find room." To his protest about the confiscation of goods from pushcarts one Saturday, the reply was, "The rabbis will thank us for this." Czerniakow said it was unfair to make the Jews bear the expense of building the wall around the ghetto because, if it was necessary to protect "Aryans" from infectious diseases, then those who benefited from that protection should pay for it. Auerswald sneered that Czerniakow should have been an international lawyer "but the Jews will pay, anyway." Pay they did, with 50 percent of the taxes collected on the ration cards.

Meanwhile the wall around the ghetto was being built higher and the ghetto area made smaller. Starvation increased. Typhus spread to such an extent that the Orthodox rabbis proposed the revival of an ancient procedure to propitiate the Almighty—the marriage of two paupers in the cemetery. Czerniakow noted this request with disgust at such superstitious nonsense.

7

Czerniakow, despite being head of the Judenrat, was not the sole authority in the Warsaw Ghetto as Rumkowski was in Lodz. Theoretically he had full power and presumably he could have tried to be as much of an autocrat as Rumkowski. Actually, as Auerswald once observed, Czerniakow was as much the ruler of the ghetto as he was king of Croatia. He tolerated—in some cases because he had no choice in the matter and in others because he chose to, believing as he did in the liberal credo of freedom of action—groups and individuals who operated for their own interests and who developed parallel power in varying degrees.

The broad spectrum of non-Judenrat authority extended from the known Gestapo agents through the House Committees to the underground political parties. The known agents, like Hendel, used the Judenrat as a source of information for their masters and sometimes brought news to Czerniakow of impending decrees. The firm of Kohn and Heller worked with the Gestapo but also served as a middleman between it and the Judenrat. The gang known as "The Thirteeners," too, had German connections; in addition, the gang concerned itself with Jewish cultural life. The Jewish Self-Help was a relief organization independent of the Judenrat and was based on House Committees. The Bund, the Communists, the Zionists of all shades carried on their own activities, frequently anti-Judenrat.

The ghetto population was well aware of the existence of informers and spies in their midst. Many a merchant would be paid a visit by the Gestapo and his carefully concealed stock confiscated. A prosperous smuggling gang would suddenly be liquidated. The Gestapo agents lived well; they had no fear of starvation, for their masters took good care of them. They simply ignored the Judenrat, paying no taxes, coming and going as they pleased. And in turn the Judenrat ignored them. What had the Judenrat to fear? It regarded itself as a body to carry out orders of the Germans, not to spy for them. If the dancer Franciska Manuvna or the boxer Anders informed the Gestapo that So-and-So had diamonds or gold hidden under his mattress, too bad for So-and-So. His fate would be a lesson to others who contravened authority and thus endangered all the Jews.

One of the Gestapo agents was a thorn in Czerniakow's side. Dr. Alfred Nossig's appointment to the Judenrat had been forced on the chairman by the Germans. Nossig did nothing but collect his salary and act as informer. Czerniakow was intolerant, not of his Gestapo connections, but of his gross inefficiency as head of a department. Exasperated, one day he fired Nossig, only to have the Germans order reinstatement the next day.

Hendel was another Gestapo agent with whom Czerniakow often met. Hendel was a personal friend of Czerniakow's and kept him informed of German plans. The Jews who acted as German agents in the ghetto were not all under one control. Some were part of the SS apparatus, some reported to the Gestapo, and some were connected with the civilian government. The bureaucratic infighting among the several German authorities was reflected in the ghetto, particularly in the case of The Thirteeners.

The Thirteeners, so called because of their headquarters at 13 Leszno Street, were headed by Abraham Ganzweich. Ganzweich originally came from Lodz; besides being an ordained rabbi, he had a good general education, having gone through six classes of *gymnasium*. His intimate friend was a German named Ollenbusch, who had worked with him on the anti-Nazi publication, *Justice*, in Vienna before the Austro-German *Anschluss*; Ollenbusch was then a Nazi agent playing the role of an antifascist. Ollenbusch had a real love for Ganzweich and went out of his way to see that no harm would come to his friend. After the conquest of Poland, Ollenbusch became Minister of Information and Propaganda in Frank's cabinet in Krakow—and Ganzweich appeared in the Warsaw Ghetto.

He opened an "Office to Fight Corruption and Speculation," ostensibly aimed at exposing and bringing to justice thieves and grafters in high places. His lieutenants were Sternfeld, Kohn, and Heller. Ganzweich had a large staff and a special police force whose officers wore dark green caps decorated with gold stars and who paraded around in well-made capes and good leather boots; his recruits came from the Jewish underworld. He organized an Emergency Squad, with red hats and gold stars; the Emergency Squad had a well-equipped ambulance.

The ambulance had another purpose than medical aid. It was convenient for carrying smuggled goods in and out of the ghetto. The Thirteeners soon had almost a monopoly on large-scale smuggling. All they had to do was threaten the existing big gangs of smugglers with being turned over to the Gestapo and they had a piece of the business. More often, in the name of the Office to Fight Corruption and Speculation they confiscated the smuggled goods unless they were paid off in merchandise or cash.

Ganzweich and his Thirteeners became a power in the ghetto. It was known that they had amicable relations with the Gestapo, that they had connections with Germans in high places, that they informed on Jews living under false names in "Aryan" Warsaw, and yet Ganzweich and his Thirteeners were treated with respect. A commentator said, "They conceal their ugly work under a veil of decency and charity." For charitable Ganzweich was. He gave free bread to the starving, bread his goons had strong-armed from the bakers. He supported circles of Chassidic students and their rabbis. He offered to subsidize the artists and writers. He worked hard to arrange for Jews to go to Palestine. He intervened to get imprisoned Jews out of jail; it was he who managed to get the famous pediatrician, Dr. Janusz Korczak, released from his six-months' sentence for going without an armband.

Of course, all that benevolence was expensive. The wherewithal came from his widespread network of legal and illegal enterprises. His interventions, not always successful or even carried out, cost a great deal of money. He had the Gestapo put pressure on the Judenrat to make him administrator (and rent-collector) of hundreds of houses in the ghetto. Under the protection of the Germans he opened new workshops in the ghetto to work for the Wehrmacht. Yet, despite his gangsterism and collaborationism, the people of the ghetto regarded him as sort of a Robin Hood; many said that he would be better than Czerniakow as head of the Judenrat because his liaison with the Germans was better and he had a greater feeling for the people's needs.

At first Czerniakow paid no attention to Ganzweich. When a German civil official asked him what he knew about the Office to Fight Corruption and Speculation, Czerniakow answered that since he had had no instructions about its head, he had opened no relations with him. He could not long ignore Ganzweich. The news was bruited around that the Germans were thinking of giving Czerniakow the title of mayor of the Jewish enclave in Warsaw. Ganzweich said publicly that Czerniakow was not worthy of being the mayor. Ganzweich gave an all-night party to which many members of the Judenrat came. There he belittled the activities of the Judenrat, especially in the social and cultural fields. He said that he would open his own workshops; in addition, he would revitalize true Jewish culture in the ghetto. A few days later Ganzweich and Sternfeld disparaged Czerniakow to SS-Oberstürmführer Rudolf Scherer, in charge of Eichmann's Section IV-B in Warsaw, saying that Czerniakow was an incompetent. Scherer, at that time in a bureaucratic struggle with the General-Gouvernement and other agencies, replied by saying that the Jewish community would not last ten days if The Thirteeners ran it. The conversation was reported to Czerniakow. Naturally, when one of Ganzweich's men asked a few days later for a post with the cultural department, Czerniakow said no.

Hendel, a regular attendant at Ganzweich's parties, carried back to Czerniakow tales of Ganzweich's increasing fulminations against the do-nothing Judenrat. Czerniakow went to Auerswald to inquire about his status. Auerswald put him off but conferred on him the title of mayor.

The title carried nothing with it. The hospitals had no food. Bread carts leaving the bakeries had to be covered with barbed wire to prevent stealing. Over 100 persons died daily, purely of starvation; the research project on starvation disease was overwhelmed with material. The Jewish police extended their press gangs, kidnapping Jews for forced labor for new airfields and military barracks. Hatred for the Judenrat grew. Czerniakow was spat at and cursed on the steps of the Judenrat building.

And all the time The Thirteeners carried on their anti-Judenrat campaign, and all the time the conflict between various German agencies continued, with the Judenrat and The Thirteeners and, of course, all the Jews expendable pawns in the deadly game. Czerniakow was asked by a Gestapo official whether Kohn and Heller were part of The Thirteeners and what they were doing. He complained to another authority that he could not issue so many permits to one firm (Kohn and Heller) because that was contrary to sound business principles. Counterattacking, another official forbade Hendel to appear at the Transfer Office. Palfinger, the head of the Transfer Office, wanted all Kohn and Heller enterprises liquidated because they made complaints about the Judenrat. Auerswald said that the Judenrat was in such disrespect that it should be reconstituted, meaning that The Thirteeners should take over. On orders from above, however, he changed his tune. He informed Czerniakow that The Thirteeners would come under the supervision of the Judenrat but that Ganzweich would have to be part of the administrative apparatus. Ganzweich wrote a letter to Czerniakow asking to be so accepted. Czerniakow snubbed him. Ganzweich offered to integrate his police into the Jewish police, provided that The Thirteeners could set up an office for price control in every section of the ghetto. Turned down, he threatened to go to Auerswald. At the Gestapo, Czerniakow was told The Thirteeners had no official backing. The Byzantine intrigues went on for several months. During that time a number of Judenrat officials, fearful of continuing in shaky posts, resigned. Czerniakow sneered at them and continued as Chairman and Mayor.

Czerniakow kept trying to discredit Ganzweich. Czerniakow had allies in the Jewish police, who felt themselves threatened by The Thirteeners' para-official force. They were on the lookout for some way to break up The Thirteeners. At last they succeeded, mainly because of dissension in the ranks of their opponents. The police had proof that Sternfeld was selling posts in The Thirteeners' police force for cash which he then pocketed. Confronted with the evidence and fearful of what Ganzweich would do, Sternfeld carried on negotiations with the Judenrat, and the Judenrat with other German authorities and Kohn and Heller. As a result, The Thirteeners' police was abolished; 100 men were taken into the Jewish police, and the remainder went into the Emergency Squad. Sternfeld himself fled to "Aryan" Warsaw. By this time the alliance between the Judenrat and the firm of Kohn and Heller was stronger than Ganzweich. His Office to Fight Corruption and Speculation was closed, and all his enterprises taken over. He was left only the house administrations. Czerniakow's pride had been piqued by the public adulation of Ganzweich, but once the gangster's power was diminished, he forgot about him. Not so Kohn and Heller. They wanted Ganzweich out of the way altogether. On the night of April 17, 1942, when the Germans arrested and shot "dangerous elements," they also arrested the remnants of Ganzweich's gang and shot them. Ganzweich, however, had been warned by an anonymous phone call on the morning of that day that he was in danger. He escaped into "Aryan" Warsaw.

Sternfeld, Kohn, and Heller, the trio that originally ran Ganzweich's apparatus, were men of the Lodz underworld. Kohn and Heller's specialty was breaking into the homes of the rich and threatening them with revolvers unless they paid out cash for the relief of the poor. As was to be expected, most of the cash stuck to their fingers. That was not enough for them. They objected to Ganzweich's open-handedness and to the expense of his philanthropies. Their objections led to arguments and finally to an open break with Ganzweich. The treasury of The Thirteeners was divided (Sternfeld was gone by now); Kohn and Heller became an independent firm. They immediately opened a private warehouse for the exchange of goods; they took over several factories from Ganzweich; they got a concession from the Germans to run horse-cars instead of the forbidden trolleys. Unlike Ganzweich, they did not seek respect from the Jewish masses. They gave charity, it is true, but in a niggardly fashion. Again unlike Ganzweich, they cooperated with the Judenrat. It was Kohn and Heller who, early in July, 1942, came to Czerniakow and warned him that a "resettlement" of the Jews of Warsaw was to take place as it had in Lublin. They had learned the news from Grauer, a Jewish Gestapo agent from Lodz. Czerniakow pooh-poohed the idea but tacitly allowed Kohn and Heller to negotiate with the Extermination Brigade in the name of the Judenrat. They brought back to Czerniakow the word that only 60,000 Jews were to be resettled. Czerniakow did nothing, but Kohn and Heller wanted to make sure of their own skins. Just before the proclamation of the "resettlement" edict they brought a large sum of money to the Extermination Brigade Office as ransom for themselves. The money was taken from them and they were shot on the spot. Their bodies were thrown out on the street and a garbage cart ordered to take them away.

Czerniakow may have felt powerless against Gestapo agents but he tried to prevent dilution of his power by the Jewish Self-Help and its House Committees. The Jewish Self-Help was a voluntary relief organization already well functioning in August, 1940. Its self-appointed task was to see that no one (especially the refugees) went without food or clothing. Its funds came through a network of solicitors who appealed to Jews on the basis of their traditions of mercy, charity, and justice. After the ghetto was closed, a more formal arrangement appeared. Each house (a complex built around a courtyard) set up its own House Committee with so many subcommittees that every family was represented on at least one. Each House Committee, primarily responsible for its own complex, saw to it within the limits of its resources that clothing and food were available, that some form of education was provided for the children, and that sanitation rules were enforced. Payment was made in cash, food, cooked meals, and clothing. Each House Committee put aside its own special emergency fund and contributed to the general treasury of the Jewish Self-Help. By November, 1940, the Jewish Self-Help had a steady income of 100,000 zlotys a month.

The Judenrat paid no attention to the idealists of the Jewish Self-Help until the House Committees became the political forum in which the anger of the masses was freely expressed as hunger and typhus spread throughout the ghetto. The House Committees argued that if the principle of collective responsibility could be adhered to by the Jewish Self-Help, then there was no reason why the Judenrat should not apply sanctions, even imprisonment, to the rich in order to get enough money for relief. If the Self-Help could collect 150,000 zlotys a month (March, 1941) from voluntary contributions, then surely the Judenrat could get more.

Czerniakow made several attempts, straightforward and devious, to coopt the Jewish Self-Help into his own bureaucracy. He pointed out to its leaders that its staff was growing and with that growth came the same corruption the Judenrat officials were accused of. Czerniakow was right: the soup kitchens showed favoritism, spent more and more, and served fewer meals; the upper levels of the staff became divorced from its broad base in the House Committees. In May, 1941, Czerniakow asked the House Committees to become responsible for quotas for the forced labor projects; the top officials agreed but had to withdraw the agreement in face of the violent opposition from below. Czerniakow then gave orders: House Committee members began to be arrested for previously overlooked violations of Judenrat regulations, like not paying taxes on time or not informing the Health Department of a case of contagious disease. From then on, candidates and volunteers for the honorary and onerous posts of House Committee members became fewer; the House Committees began to decline in influence and its collectors were evaded.

Further pressure on the Jewish Self-Help was applied by the delay in the winter relief campaign of 1941-1942. The Judenrat was very conscious of the hatred for it felt by the masses. Czerniakow hoped to dilute that hatred by getting the Jewish Self-Help to work with it in the campaign. He found a way. In January, 1942, the Germans ordered that all furs in the ghetto be turned over to them without payment therefor. Immediately furs were sold sub rosa to Poles, given away to street children, and sliced or otherwise damaged so the Germans could not use them. Disappointed by the poor response, the Germans offered to set free those Jews awaiting execution for leaving the ghetto without a pass in exchange for 1,500 intact furs or their equivalent. The Judenrat wanted the House Committees to aid in the collection, but the latter refused because that would be aiding the enemy; Jewish Self-Help officials prevailed on the House Committees to change their minds because the Jews could regard the collection as a forced contribution to help save the lives of other Jews. The fur collections and the Winter Relief campaign were combined and were successful.

Elated by the result and coming at last to the conclusion that he could solve the financial problems of the Judenrat by increasing special taxes on the wealthy, Czerniakow proposed such measures to his associates. They would not consider them. The dictator Rumkowski ignored his Advisory Council; Czerniakow felt bound by its will.

Probably no amount of money could overcome the spreading starvation. The customary methods of collection for the House Committees failed. They began to have weekly entertainments to raise money; they organized dozens of little card clubs whose kitty went to the House Committees. In high dudgeon Czerniakow said gambling was bad for the morale of the ghetto. He ordered high license fees to be charged for the use of halls for the entertainments; his police raided the card clubs and confiscated the money they found. Nevertheless, the Jewish Self-Help and its House Committees limped along. Czerniakow then tried a direct approach. In April, 1942, he ordered the Jewish Self-Help to be incorporated into his administration "by order of the Germans." A howl went up from the House Committees. "Better dissolve than join!" Czerniakow was forced to back down. He was aggrieved and expressed his vexation in a talk with Jonas Turkow, the representative of the cultural section of the Jewish Self-Help, which had just refused to unite with the redesigned cultural section of the Judenrat. "Everything that would bring respect and honor you want for the Jewish Self-Help and you leave us the hard bone of unpopularity to chew on because we—you say—are police officials. Then you come from the Jewish Self-Help and criticize us for our needed but unpopular work. I have the authority to force you to work for us but I won't use that authority. Nevertheless, I'll not tolerate two artists' associations in the ghetto." A considerable correspondence ensued about unification, a correspondence that terminated with the events of July, 1942.

8

From the very beginning of the closed ghetto, the political parties ignored the ban on their activities and carried on illegally. Secret meetings were held, underground publications circulated, resistance to the Germans advocated. What was meant by resistance ranged from general anti-fascist slogans to training units for guerrilla warfare. Czerniakow suggested at first, then demanded that the leaders of the parties (Bund, Communists, Zionists) cooperate with advice and with the execution of Judenrat decisions. In his discussions with them he reiterated his contention that the party leaders had abandoned their responsibility to the people, leaving him holding the bag and being blamed for every misfortune that befell the Jews. He told the leaders he was not at all averse to playing a minor role if they would participate in the government of the Jewish community; he said he did not consider himself as the guide or head of the Jews but rather as a man thrown to the forefront by circumstances. No parties took on formal administrative activities, but some leaders agreed to work with Judenrat committees. Later, as the Judenrat became the target of widespread ghetto criticism, they left their posts lest they be accused of being contaminated by the Council's corruption. Czerniakow resented the respect given to the party leaders but understood why it was given: "They don't do much but also they're not part of the Judenrat."

As was to be expected, the parties of the left attacked Czerniakow and the Judenrat for being compliant agents of the Germans and for the class character of the means they used to cope with the problems of the masses—overcrowding, disease, and above all, hunger.

Czerniakow was consistent in his policy. He felt he was merely a transmission belt for German orders, an office-holder carrying out decisions from above, not a satrap with discretionary powers. He published the German decree forbidding political activities, but he made no attempt to suppress them. That was not his job. If foolish hotheads persisted in their folly, the Germans would take care of them. The raids that extreme left-wingers organized on the clubs and restaurants of the wealthy, even the several attacks on the Jewish police in 1941, brought warnings from him but no reprisals. When the underground press assailed him because of the tax system that bore most heavily on the poor, Czerniakow replied that an income tax was ridiculous, no one in the ghetto having any income. Technically that was true. The wealthy had assets that they sold off so that they could live well, but that was not income in the sense of profit. Czerniakow was asked to make a capital levy based on the living standard of the rich. He said a capital levy was out of the question on theoretical and practical grounds. It would violate the principle of equality among the Jews and it could be easily evaded. The underground press said he should apply sanctions against tax evaders, but Czerniakow answered that he was not the one to pass judgment on other Jews—they had trouble enough already. Demonstrations against the forced labor occurred several times. Czerniakow ignored the demonstrations as stupid. He could do nothing but follow German orders.

And indeed, the demonstrations brought no changes. The underground was divided; there was no organized unifying group advocating sabotage or armed resistance until the spring of 1942. In March of that year the Anti-Fascist Bloc (made up of Young Zionist groups, Labor Zionists, and Communists) began to formulate plans to fight the Germans. In April the Revisionists (right-wing Zionists) began to train a cadre for guerrilla activity.

The Germans were ready for any interference with their plans. In the early morning hours of April 18, 1942, the Gestapo took fifty-two Jews from their homes and shot them in the street outside the courtyards. Besides The Thirteeners' gang, the killed included communal and cultural leaders involved in the underground, Bundists, Young Zionists, Communists, printers, and bakers. The last two were the most important financial backers of the resistance movement. The Anti-Fascist Bloc was severely shaken, and before it could gain more recruits and mobilize its forces came the great July purge of the Jews.

Czerniakow was frightened by the killings. He notified the heads of the political parties that they were on a dangerous path. He said the killings arose from their illegal publications and secret meetings. All talk of resistance must be stopped. Any open resistance or sabotage of materials destined for the Germans would be an excuse for the conquerors to apply the principle of collective responsibility, and the reprisals might go so far as to lead to the wholesale deportation of the Jews of Warsaw.

His pleas for passivity were unheeded. In June, 1942, Auerswald ordered 110 Jews to be taken from the prison and shot as a warning to the ghetto to "cease acts of terrorism and disobedience of orders."

9

Much justification existed for the hatred the Left felt for the Judenrat. "All are equal" actually meant that the poor, being greater in number, bore the heaviest burden of taxes. For the first six months of 1942, the Judenrat collected from refugees for their shelter 412,000 zlotys, for hospital charges 900,000 zlotys, and for ration card fees 4,567,000 zlotys. The rations themselves supplied a calorie intake at famine level, and even then they were unfairly apportioned—1,500 calories for Judenrat employees, 1,000 for workers and professionals, 300 for all others. The cost of the rations was determined by the free market, hence was staggeringly high. Over 20 percent of the poor were unable to buy the products listed on the ration cards; they sold their cards on the street or to the House Committees for cash to buy bread or potatoes or whatever else they could afford. Deaths from starvation increased so alarmingly that the Judenrat had to issue extra bread ration cards: for the police—12 kilograms, for the Judenrat bureaucracy—4 kilos, for workers—6 kilos. But the extra ration was again at the expense of the sick, the refugees, and the unemployed, a half kilo being taken from their rations to make up for what was given the others. The ghetto masses said bitterly, "The Germans destroy us, but first the Judenrat tortures us."

German manufacturers opened branch factories in the ghetto. They paid nothing, but they found plenty of workers willing to work for the hot lunch of soup and bread they served. New Jewish workshops appeared and had to turn away hundreds of applicants for jobs; everyone sought work, even for the most meager wage, because the slightest increase in family income meant the difference between life and death from starvation. Those who still had money also began to look for work. The news of the liquidation of the small provincial ghettos led to rumors that soon the Warsaw Ghetto would be cleared of all but productive workers, and all others would be deported "to the East for resettlement." Czerniakow vigorously attacked the rumor-mongers, but he did not suppress his own opinion that Jewish productivity in the ghetto was one of the reasons the Germans permitted the existence of such an "autonomous area."

Meanwhile starvation continued. The cost of bread and potatoes rose. Smuggling became an increasingly important factor in maintaining the life of the ghetto. Food to the value of 1,800,000 zlotys was legally brought into the ghetto, but between 70 and 80 million zlotys worth was smuggled in. Five to six hundred Jews died daily of starvation; 35 percent of the population had hunger edema.

The corruption of Judenrat officialdom became more open. The Jewish cemetery lay outside the ghetto walls; the Judenrat charged a fee of 2-1/2 zlotys to go there, and as many as could go went, not to say Kaddish for the dead but to contact "Aryan" smugglers to barter their last possessions for an egg (7 zlotys) or a kilogram of horse meat (35 zlotys). Of course, the Jewish police got a rake-off on every transaction. And when the Germans wanted 400 young men, the Jewish police rounded up 800 in one night. The families of the extra 400 had to pay ransom for their release. Czerniakow knew of the corruption but did little about it except order the arrest of a few clerks. He excused his inaction by saying that his legal advisers said the evidence was too slim to prosecute the offenders.

The Germans demanded more men for construction work at Treblinka, about fifty miles northeast of Warsaw. Czerniakow told them that Jews were better suited for factory work than for outside labor, but the men were taken anyway. Czerniakow commented in his diary on the German mania for building; he was unaware of what was being built at Treblinka—gas chambers and crematoria. Auerswald must have laughed up his sleeve at Czerniakow's credulity. He refused to initial an order for special taxes to support the families of those sent to work at Treblinka; to Czerniakow's objection that for two years such a signature had been a mere formality, Auerswald replied that for the next five years a new procedure would be followed. Czerniakow took the remark as evidence of the continuance of the ghetto.

Czerniakow, like Rumkowski, also regarded the importation of non-Polish Jews as another safeguard for the ghetto. Several thousand German Jews were sent in. Ghetto dwellings were emptied of their tenants to make room for them, but no increase in rations was allowed to the ghetto. Czerniakow extended himself to see that the German Jews were taken care of. He permitted a Protestant (Jewish) minister to hold prayer meetings. He ordered a group of German Jewish workers to get cigarettes, extra pay, and a supplementary half loaf of bread daily, commenting, "The efficiency and gratitude shown by the German Jews should be an example to our Jews."

At last Czerniakow began to take measures against the rich. Police raided stores and confiscated such luxuries as lard, sardines, chocolate, and cookies; they took the lion's share and sent the rest to the refugee points. Czerniakow said he sympathized with the police because their wages were so low. When Police Chief Szerynski was arrested, Czerniakow feared for the demoralization of the police. The time was bad for that; unrest needed a force for law and order. At the end of April new maps and population statistics had been ordered; Czerniakow saw in the requests the possibility of an evacuation of much of the ghetto area. Hendel reported to him that military officials and others were having meetings about the ghetto. A few days later, Czerniakow was ordered to supply a report about the number of actual workers; to him this meant that unproductive workers would be evacuated.

Nevertheless, he sought to hearten the ghetto Jews. In a speech in May at the opening of a new playground for children, he said, "These are tragic times, but we must stand firm. It is surely more than coincidental that the playground should be directly opposite the Judenrat building. Whenever we hear children laughing and singing, our windows will be open to let in the sound. This will give us hope and courage to go and fight for the future." He announced that a new training school for teachers and a ballet school for girls would soon be opened. The speech impressed no one. Dr. Korczak called the whole ceremony a *Purimspiel,* a burlesque.

Word began to trickle into the ghetto that the liquidation of the provincial ghettos meant extermination, not deportation and resettlement on a Jewish reservation. More rumors about an evacuation from Warsaw spread, and with them fear, and with fear the illusion that a "productive ghetto" meant safety. When, in June, 1942, the Germans issued an order that everyone would have to have new identification cards with photographs, a sigh of relief went up from the ghetto. The logically thinking Jews reasoned that that was proof the ghetto would not be liquidated because the Germans wouldn't waste time on such nonsense if they were going to move out all the Jews, anyway. Czerniakow paid no attention to the story that 70,000 Jews were to be removed. He had inquired and the Germans had assured him of the absurdity of such a story. He wondered, just the same, when he was ordered to set up a special reserve fund. "What emergency is expected?" he wrote in his diary.

He also noted that "slimy characters" like the informer Ehrlich were worrying about their future. He implied that they were no longer trusting their German masters. He also noted the disappearance from the ghetto of a number of wealthy individuals; presumably they had fled to "Aryan" Warsaw.

His anxiety increased. He called a special meeting of selected Jewish leaders at his apartment on July 1, 1942. There he spoke out boldly about the Germans' barbarous treatment of the Jews and opened the discussion on what could be done (not resistance!) to counteract that barbarism. The meeting closed, consistent with Czerniakow's Polishness, with the playing of Chopin's music and the singing of the Polish national anthem.

The German mechanism for "the final solution of the Jewish problem" went into full gear. Starting on July 15, Estonians, Letts, Lithuanians, and Ukrainians reinforced and gradually replaced the Polish guards around the ghetto walls. The next day all Jews with valid foreign passports as proof they were not Polish citizens were ordered to report to the prison in the ghetto; they were allowed to take with them 20 zlotys and a valise weighing no more than ten kilograms. It was rumored that they were to be sent to Switzerland if they came from neutral countries or held for exchange for German nationals interned in Allied countries.

Czerniakow took Kohn and Heller's warning about the coming "resettlement" lightly. He conferred with Brandt and Scherer and other German officials and then issued a categorical denial of any plans for "resettlement." The Germans even threatened an investigation of the source of such lies. Much as they hated the Judenrat, the ghetto populace, nervous and panicky because of the rumors, this time preferred to believe Czerniakow rather than the so-called insiders.

More evacuees from the provinces were pushed into the ghetto, more men were taken to work at Treblinka, more people died of starvation, and more concerts were given. Criticized for permitting entertainments during such a perilous time, Czerniakow replied, "I am like the captain of a sinking ship who orders the band to play to calm the passengers."

The offhand remark was more accurate than he knew. On July 21, Brandt and Captain Hoefle of the Einsatz Reinhard Extermination Brigade visited Czerniakow to tell him that 6,000 Jews would be deported daily for the next ten days. The Judenrat could select who was to go. If they refused to do so, the Germans would take over. The entire Judenrat, except for Czerniakow and the attorney Gustav Wielokowski, were taken as hostages to ensure the absence of "incidents." Czerniakow was cool and calm during the conference. The two officers presented him for his signature a petition asking them to remove all nonproductive Jews from the ghetto. He refused to sign. The Judenrat members in prison all signed the petition and were freed.

Czerniakow called an emergency meeting of all organizations in the ghetto. He warned them that if the Germans entered the ghetto not deportation but slaughter would take place. He asked for their full cooperation, especially from the Jewish Self-Help.

He asked the latter group to help fill the daily quotas and to aid in provisioning the deportees. The Jewish Self-Help agreed. The House Committees objected feebly but gave in.

On the morning of July 22, placards announcing the "resettlement" were put up. Starting that day, all Jews in Warsaw regardless of age or sex were to be "resettled" in the East. Exemptions were many: Jews employed by German military and civil authorities and enterprises, Jews employed making goods for the Germans, Judenrat employees of all grades (including the Jewish Self-Help), Jews engaged in any branch of health activity, all wives and children of the fore-named categories. In keeping with the "Aryan cunning" which the Germans used to deceive the Jews, the deportees were allowed to take with them personal effects weighing not more than fifteen kilograms and any gold, silver, or jewelry they had. Penalty for evasion or resistance to the order was shooting on the spot. The order was signed by "The Judenrat of Warsaw," not by Czerniakow. Czerniakow himself was told that his wife would be shot were the evacuation to meet any resistance.

Early the next morning the Germans took away Czerniakow's automobile, the symbol of his authority. The ghetto was in wild panic. The Jewish police were dragging deportees to the Umschlagsplatz where they were loaded into freight cars supposedly going to the East, but actually to the death camp at Treblinka. Germans and their Ukrainian and Baltic auxiliaries shot people on the slightest pretext.

Czerniakow was at the Judenrat building all day (the 23rd). During the morning he conferred with Worthoff, the German officer in charge of the evacuation team, wangling exemptions for students in the vocational schools and for husbands of working women. He was told the evacuation would last a week. In the afternoon he wrote in his diary, "It is now three o'clock. So far 4,000 have been taken for evacuation. By four o'clock 4,000 more will go. Some clerks came to the [ghetto] post office and ordered that all incoming letters and packages should be sent to Pawiak [the prison]." That was the last entry in the diary.

A short time later, Czerniakow rang for his secretary to bring him a glass of water. He was pale and shivering. He thanked her and dismissed her for the rest of the day. About ten minutes later the phone began to ring in his office. A Judenrat employee in another office wondered why Czerniakow did not answer the phone. He opened the door and saw Czerniakow slumped over his desk, dead. On the desk was an empty vial of potassium cyanide and a half glass of water. Nearby were two short notes. One was a farewell to his wife, asking her to forgive him for leaving her. The other was to the Judenrat, saying that Worthoff had said that the expulsion order applied to children, too. He could not hand over helpless children for destruction. He had therefore decided to put an end to his life. That should not be regarded as an act of cowardice. "I am powerless. My heart trembles in sorrow and pity. I can no longer bear all this. My act will prove to everyone what is the right thing to do." On a pad nearby was "Ten thousand ordered for tomorrow and seven thousand thereafter—" and then two illegible words.

He was buried at five-thirty the next morning. The Germans had ordered that no large funeral be held. Barely more than the *minyan* (religious quorum) were present. Someone said the Kaddish (not his only son, then serving in the Red Army). At the graveside Dr. Janusz Korczak, who himself was to go to Treblinka with his children from the orphanage a few weeks later, gave the eulogy. He concluded with, "The Lord entrusted you with the honorable task of watching over the dignity of the Jewish people. Now you are honored to bring it back to the Lord!"

10

The news of Czerniakow's suicide had a sharp impact on the mass of terror-stricken Jews. They saw in it an omen of evil to come, but they did not realize how horrible an evil. In the short space of two months 300,000 Jews from Warsaw were sent off to the gas chambers at Treblinka. Only 70,000 were left. Now there was no overcrowding. Apartments were vacant, their contents systematically looted by the Germans. The ghetto area was cut down. By the end of the expulsion the remaining Jews had proof that their friends, neighbors, and relatives had been killed en masse.

Everyone left worked for German firms. The Judenrat, now headed by Marek Lichtenboim, had little to do but publish German decrees. Even that function was nominal. It had not the power to enforce them. The Jews resisted, first passively and then actively, as they forged a relative unity against the oppressors.

In January, 1943, Himmler ordered the ghetto to be completely liquidated. By that time, however, the Jewish Fighting Organization (*Zhob*) was prepared. It successfully fought off the Germans. The ghetto limped on.

The end was only a matter of time. In April, 1943, other measures having failed, the Germans started an open military action against the ghetto. *Zhob* fought back fiercely but, poorly armed as it was and overwhelmed by the masses of German infantry and artillery, the revolt was doomed. But the Germans did not have an easy job. The operation that was to have lasted three days took over a month. On May 16, General Stroop was able to report that "the Jewish Residential District no longer exists . . . Where dynamiting was not used, only fire walls remain standing." He said that 56,065 Jews were captured, of whom 7,000 were killed at once and 6,929 at Treblinka, plus 5,000 or 6,000 more by being blown up or burned. And yet surviving groups still fought on in the smoking ruins. Not until September, 1943, could it be said that no Jews remained in the Warsaw Ghetto, now a pile of rubble, a silent, deserted wasteland.

11

Ghetto opinion, then and later, was divided about the meaning of Czerniakow's suicide and his role as chairman. Some said his suicide was unworthy of a leader and fruitless, besides; he should have shared with the ghetto his certain knowledge that "resettlement" was a euphemism for death, that no compromise with the Germans was possible, and that resistance was the only course left. Others said that he functioned as chairman of the Judenrat only because he felt that he could, even in a small way, help the

Jews to survive; when that possibility evaporated, he took his life. Some said that he meant his suicide to be a signal that fearful times lay ahead for the Jews; others, that he could not bring himself to be responsible for the murder of his brethren. Representative comments follow.

Dr. Hillel Seidman, journalist: Czerniakow's suicide was an act of heroism.

Marek Edelman, Bundist leader: Czerniakow knew beyond a doubt that the supposed deportation to the East meant death, and he refused to assume responsibility. Unable to counteract events, he decided to quit altogether. . . . We thought he had no right to act as he did. We thought that since he was the only person in the ghetto whose voice carried a great deal of authority, it was his duty to inform the entire population of the state of affairs and also to dissolve all public bodies, particularly the Jewish police, which had been established by the Judenrat and was legally subservient to it.

Dr. Emanuel Ringelblum, the underground archivist: Too late—a sign of weakness—should have called for resistance—a weak man.

Noëmi Szac-Wajnkranc, a Jewish woman of the Polish intelligentsia: Czerniakow . . . twisted and turned like a fish in a net; he kept trying to repair the ever-increasingly broken life in the ghetto until he was forced one day to understand that such repair was impossible. He took cyanide. He committed suicide because he could not agree to the plans laid before him to liquidate the ghetto, because he would not take on himself to send human beings to death. Maybe he wanted his action to be a signal for an uprising on our part. Through his death we were to have understood that the last moment drew near, that we had nothing to lose.

* * *

Dr. Nathan Eck, organizer of the House Committees: [Activists] charged the Judenrat with negligence, inefficiency, lack of resolution, and cowardice. Certain members of the Judenrat were also suspected of being responsible for acts of injustice, of getting rich at public expense, etc. As against these, the chairman, Czerniakow, was accepted and even liked by the people. He was regarded as an upright and sincere man, well intentioned, who did not seek public office, but on the contrary, had been compelled to accept the position he held by the Nazis, and his plight was far more dangerous than that of ordinary members of the Jewish public. The fact that he was considered a mediocre figure, devoid of any brilliant talents and unendowed with the necessary resolution did not diminish the regard in which he was held. Indeed, it may have enhanced it. . . . Czerniakow never could have been nor did he want to be the Führer of the ghetto . . .

Dr. Chaim Kaplan, educator: The first victim of the expulsion decree was the chairman, Adam Czerniakow. . . . His end perpetuated his name more than his life. His end proves conclusively that he worked and strove for the good of his people, that he wanted its welfare and continuity even though everything done in his name was not praiseworthy. The expulsion decree . . . was not signed in the usual manner of Judenrat notices, "Head of the Judenrat, Certified Engineer Adam Czerniakow," but merely, "Judenrat." This innovation astonished those circles who examine bureaucratic changes in notices. After the chairman's death, the reason became clear. Czerniakow had refused to sign the expulsion order. He followed the Talmudic law: If someone comes to kill me, using might and main and turning a deaf ear to all my pleas, he can do to me whatever his heart desires since he has the power, and strength always prevails. But to give my consent, to sign my own death warrant—this no power on earth can force me to do, not even the brutal force of the foul-souled Nazi.

Joshua Perle, journalist: Czerniakow was a man of insignificant spiritual stature, a thoroughly assimilated Jewish intellectual. The cruel hand of fate decreed that he should be placed at the head of the largest Jewish community in Europe at a time which was unparalleled in the annals of history. This engineer was not equal to the great and simultaneously tragic role in which he had been cast. It was beyond his strength as well as beyond his power of comprehension to understand the responsibility of the office he had assumed. He led the Warsaw Jewish community as would a man with a limited viewpoint, and what is worse, showed his fear and timidity openly. All that Hitler's bandits demanded of him he granted. Never did he dare to speak in a tone that indicated more than ordinary unconcern, and never did he dare to show opposition to the slightest degree. He felt that by his methods he would be able to save that which could be saved. He saved nothing; neither he nor any of the other members of the Judenrat who crawled to the Germans on all fours. . . . Czerniakow went to his eternal rest, and while his body was still warm, the Jewish police were already on the streets carrying out their master's plans.

Yitzhak Katzenelson, the poet, in his Song of the Slaughtered Jewish People: Czerniakow, the traitor, knew the Angel of Death was waiting for the deportees and he kept his mouth shut.

Mordecai Tanenbaum, an inhabitant of the Warsaw Ghetto who left it and became head of the resistance movement in the Bialystok Ghetto: I know only three honorable men who were chairmen of Judenrat. One was Czerniakow. . . .

Ludwik Herszfeld, professor of immunology and serology: The members of the Judenrat, with few exceptions, did not enjoy a good reputation. It is not for me to judge whether this was deserved. Once I spoke about this to the chairman of the Judenrat, Mr. Czerniakow, on whom no shadow of suspicion of acting from motives of self-interest ever fell. He told me that highly educated individuals went to pieces in this tragedy and that only those with nerves of steel kept their composure. Only those were capable of assuming posts of command and responsibility, and such hardness seldom went hand in hand with a sensitive conscience. . . .

Michel Mazor, writer, himself a deportee: Czerniakow was not a collaborator in the sense that the word is ordinarily used, meaning one who got personal favors from the Germans, but merely a man who carried out German orders.

Jonas Turkow, actor: Czerniakow was an honest and upright man. No one could throw up to him that he, like many other members of the Judenrat, collaborated with the Germans to sell out his people. . . . He was a weak character and a poor judge of people so that the Judenrat became an institution of graft, corruption, and favoritism, with people in it who sucked like leeches on the organism of the Jewish masses. He was caught in the web spun by his "efficient" functionaries. . . . As head of the Judenrat he took on a very responsible and thankless task. He was unequal to it. . . . But he meant well within the limits of his capabilities. He could have left Warsaw to go abroad—he had a ready foreign passport, but he said no. Maybe he thought his life was not in danger. Maybe he thought leaving his post would be an act of treachery to the Jewish people. . . .

12

Rumkowski's personality is known to us by reflection in the mirror of the speeches reported by his toadies. They excused his actions, extolled his benevolence, and magnified his "work policy" as the only valid way of survival for "his Jews." Czerniakow's actions—or inactions, depending on the reporter—were also noted in detail by many observers, friendly and unfriendly, but in addition we have a personal document which illuminates his character. Czerniakow left behind him a diary in which he noted the events of each day from the beginning of the war until the day of his death. The diary, rich in details of the difficult administrative tasks with which he was faced, also shows how he pictured himself and how he actually functioned as leader of the Jewish community of Warsaw.

He noted the daily temperature, the state of the weather, and the time he went to his office. He described his physical condition (headaches, stomach upset, lumbago, etc.). He was somewhat of a hypochondriac, a pill-taker. He was concerned that his health might suffer from his working too hard and complained that he ought to have more than the few three-day vacations he took in the country.

He was fond of reading, particularly, in belles lettres, frequently quoting Cervantes, Proust, Flaubert, and Dickens, as well as Polish writers. Striking in the diary is the absence of biblical quotations, either in Polish or Hebrew, and of any Yiddish phrases. He was almost obsessively clean in his personal habits; he disliked handling greasy or dirty books. More than once he deplored the filth in the ghetto and the indifference of the Jews about cleaning it up; he did not, however, see the reason for that indifference—the search for food was more important than sweeping the courtyards.

Together with his passion for cleanliness went a meticulous desire for exactitude. A misfiled document or index card aroused in him more indignation than the sight of hunger-swollen beggars. He recorded his anger when Auerswald accused him of being like the other Jews, "imprecise in his statistics."

The trees of administrative detail may have obscured his vision of the forest of destruction around him. His diary discusses at length the most petty arrangements in the financial field and gives only here and there a view of the death and misery around him, and then often only as the result of a complaint from the Germans. For example, he was told "it was not nice" to see dead bodies on the street; he speeded up their collection by the under-

takers' barrows. He mentioned occasionally but coldly the rising
mortality from starvation and typhus, but in spite of his liking
for literature he left no description of the horror that was the
Warsaw Ghetto.

Formally Jewish in religion, he regarded belief in ritual as
unworthy of an educated man. But as a public figure he felt he
had to avoid injuring the sensibilities of the more pious and ignorant Jews; he went to the synagogue on the High Holidays and
on those days stayed away (at least part of the day) from his office.
He felt no hypocrisy in his going to the synagogue; that to him
was bearing witness of his Jewishness.

His lack of interest in Jewish (Yiddish) culture was betokened
by the failure to comment on the wide range of cultural programs
organized by the Jewish Self-Help. Education of the young, however, was close to his heart. He spared no effort to open elementary schools and schools for vocational training, as well as
specialized classes for embryo doctors and nurses.

Smugness and self-satisfaction frequently shine through the
pages of his diary, even when he reports the curses and epithets
hurled at him in the Judenrat building. When the *Gazeta Zydowska*
(Jewish News), a paper in Polish published under German auspices,
ran an adulatory editorial about him, he wrote, "They are trying
to bribe me." He described the dignity and correctness with which
he bore himself under all circumstances and the scrupulosity with
which he carried out his official functions. He noted with pleasure
how the ghetto people looked up to him for relief from the
oppressors, how leading citizens like Gepner congratulated him
on his efficiency, how he was called "the martyr" when the SS
beat him for not reporting a radio apparatus, how others called
him "a hero of our time" and "a figure out of legend," how the
rabbis praised him for proclaiming Saturday as the weekly day
of rest. He prided himself on setting an example of asceticism:
he did not go to parties and disapproved of those who did in
such perilous times; he absented himself from the theater during
the agitation over the ill-treatment of workers in the labor camps;

he would not draw his salary while the clerks of the Judenrat were unpaid.

He was critical of Rumkowski, whom he met in May of 1941, when he came to Warsaw to recruit doctors for his health service. Rumkowski said he was appalled at the open begging in the streets; in Litzmannstadt there were no beggars in the streets. Rumkowski told Czerniakow he should rule as a Tsar without regard to individuals, keeping always in mind the great goal of saving the Jews as a whole. Czerniakow wrote of Rumkowski, "He is a very arrogant man who considers himself wise and who injures us because he babbles in front of [German] authorities how good it is in his city, and then the Germans here disbelieve what we say about our troubles."

The picture we get from his diary is that of an unsentimental, practical businessman in charge of a philanthropic organization. That was how he regarded the Judenrat, as a sort of Kehillah. That it was the transmission belt for German orders was secondary to him. The Judenrat had to promulgate and execute those orders, but its main task, he felt, was the alleviation of the distress of the Jews by the same methods used by the prewar Kehillah.

The entries in the diary, meant for himself alone, seldom mention his family in terms of warmth. Such personal feelings he evidently could not put down on paper. He describes his wife as having problems with the household budget; there is not much else about her. The day his dog disappeared (possibly it was killed and eaten, as were other dogs and cats) he comments on his sorrow at its loss and ends with, "I wonder where J [his son] is today."

Czerniakow had what Freudians might call the personality characteristics of a sublimated anal-eroticism: a desire for cleanliness, order, and petty detail. His professional education and his prewar career confirmed that bent. He regarded education as a tool, a means to get on in the world. His love of literature was the accepted sign of a cultured man. In the days he was Chairman, he remained cold and rigid, adhering to the classic work-ethic dogmas. Two days before the expulsion decree, he was concerned with the logistics of setting up a reform school for children arrested for snatching food. At a crucial time, when cheating, deception, lying, pretense, and lawbreaking were literally vitally necessary for the survival of the Jews, he refused to compromise and held fast to the old principles of honesty, hard work, and straightforwardness, principles that had lost all meaning in the walled slaughterhouse of the ghetto.

13

Can we say of Czerniakow, knowing as we do of what followed his death, that he should have done better, that meaning well was not enough, that he should have supported and encouraged resistance? Perhaps his failure in the times of crisis came from too logical a mind. Who could imagine the Germans would be so stupid as to destroy so many needed war-workers? Who could conceive that they would use indispensable rolling stock in a decisive time of the war merely to transport Jews to death camps? Perhaps he was a little too farsighted and saw ahead the total physical destruction of the Warsaw Ghetto if resistance were attempted.

Perhaps he was too scrupulous, too much of the business executive, too blinded by details. He never assumed he was a dictator over the Jews, as Rumkowski did; he functioned as head of the Judenrat just as he would have functioned as head of a commercial enterprise or as the chairman of a fund-raising charitable organization in a sane society. Perhaps he was too liberal-democratic in viewpoint to realize that ideas of progress and humanity no longer had meaning, pushed aside as they were by Hitlerism. Perhaps at the end he understood that he had nothing to substitute for his correctness and obedience to the Germans, nothing that would thwart the lethal plans of the "scientific" racists, nothing to save the Jews of Warsaw. Cold reason could not overcome the cold, rational insanity of the Germans.

Rumkowski, the vulgar megalomaniac parvenu, and Czerniakow, the hard-headed solid citizen, each tried as best he knew how to fulfill the impossible task of being a leader of the doomed. Rumkowski was a dictator; Czerniakow was an administrator. Both were deluded in different ways into thinking they could stop or slow the inexorable progress of the German extermination plan. Too late, they recognized their delusions.

Ghetto Chief
Jacob Gens

Dr. Mark Dworzhetzki, a physician in the Vilna Ghetto, wrote about Jacob Gens:

> The ghetto hated the Jewish ghetto police but it wanted to see in its commandant an honest man. Jews were happy when they heard tales of good deeds he had done. They wanted to persuade themselves, justly or unjustly, that at the head of the ghetto stood an energetic Jew whose concern was always for the welfare of the ghetto, for its defense and security. Everyone clung to the illusion that here was a man who'd watch over the ghetto, be its guardian. Such thoughts gave hope during the terror-stricken times of waiting for new purges. One would whisper to another, "Maybe Gens will maneuver to save us at the last moment? Maybe. . . ."

1

Vilna (Wilno in Polish, Vilnius in Lithuanian), the traditional capital of Lithuania, was known and honored as the Jerusalem of Lithuania among the Jews of Eastern Europe. Vilna, situated at the crossroads of Slavic and German cultures, since the fourteenth century had been a center of Judaism and was the birthplace in modern times of secular Yiddish learning and the arts. There the revered Gaon, the world-famous religious authority, had flourished; there the leaders of the Enlightenment found their first disciples; and there the Bund, the major Jewish socialist organization, was founded. Hebrew was the language of the 300 synagogues, the seminaries, the yeshivas, and the Zionist clubs; Yiddish of the vocational schools, the music conservatory, the theater, the nursery schools, and the internationally known Jewish Scientific Institute.

Vilna was an important commercial city. Lumber mills and ancillary enterprises, leather factories, linen factories, radio factories, and an oil refinery were the main industries. Vilna was the center of the fur industry in Europe, the site of the International Fur Fair.

Vilna's history since the downfall of the Tsarist regime had been checkered. Independent Lithuania, broken away from Russia, selected it as its capital in 1920, but the Polish general, Zeligowski, occupied the city and forced its transfer to Poland. The Polish regime made Polish the official language and suppressed all irredentist movements. When the Germans invaded Poland in 1939 and the Soviet army took over eastern Poland, Vilna was returned to the precariously independent Lithuanian government. On June 15, 1940, under the influence of the Red Army garrisons stationed in Lithuania, the bourgeois nationalist government was overthrown and a People's Government established. In August of the same year Lithuania became a Soviet Republic annexed to the USSR. Vilna remained the capital.

In 1931 there were 14,100 Jews in Vilna out of its total population of 50,000. Swollen by refugees from Nazi-occupied Poland, by 1941 the population reached 190,000. Of that number 100,000 were Poles, 30,000 were Lithuanians, and 60,000 were Jews. Among the Jewish refugees were prominent intellectuals and political leaders of all parties and factions. The Jews were not united by their sufferings; the Polish Jews looked down on the Litvaks, their contemptuous name for Lithuanian Jews, as no better than uncultured peasants.

Under Polish rule the Jews had been oppressed by the anti-Semitic laws, as in Lodz and Warsaw. In independent Lithuania the government rigorously enforced the laws directed against the Jewish minority: dissolution of the Community Councils, prohibition of signs in Yiddish, discrimination in licenses for foreign trade, credit restrictions, and limitation of the Jewish press. The Lithuanian Soviet Republic gave the Jews full citizenship rights but, because of the forced nationalization of commercial and industrial enterprises, a severe blow was dealt to Jewish economic life.

The Jews of Vilna were in a particularly precarious position. Nationalist Lithuanians had never forgiven them for taking an officially neutral stand in the Polish-Lithuanian conflict; other Lithuanians hated them as being supporters of the Communists; Poles regarded them as pro-Lithuanian; and the Soviet rulers were suspicious of them as *ci-devant* entrepreneurs and, in the main, followers of the anti-Soviet Bund, "unreliable elements." The Soviet government maintained the restrictions on the press. Early in June, 1941, the government deported to Siberia along with Lithuanian nationalists hundreds of politically active Jews: Bundists, Zionists, and Revisionists.

2

On June 22, 1941, the Germans invaded the Soviet Union. Vilna was attacked by bombing planes. The Soviet troops retreated. A short-lived Lithuanian government appeared, but on June 24 the Germans occupied Vilna, and a military command was set up over the city. The Vilna City Council became merely an adjunct of the German army.

No attacks on the Jews, like those in Lodz and Warsaw, took

place when the Soviet troops left. The hastily formed Lithuanian militia kept order after their own fashion. To avoid the many incidents of Jews being pushed out of the queues lined up for food, the militia ordered, "Jews in one line, Christians in another."

Disorder was introduced by the Germans. Homes of Jews were searched, ostensibly for weapons but actually to lift whatever of value the searchers could find (jewelry, silverware, *objets d'art*). If books printed in Cyrillic characters were found, even works by Dostoyevsky or Tolstoy, their presence was taken as proof of sympathy with Russian ideology and the men of the household were arrested and carted off to prison.

On June 27, three days later, "snatching" began. Jewish men walking the streets were seized, temporarily jailed, and from the jail removed in buses "for work outside the city." Only workers with notes stating they worked for Germans were released. The work outside the city was presumed to be the building of a highway or of military barracks near the Ponary woods, about twelve kilometers from Vilna; the sound of gunfire from the area was interpreted as target practice. Snatching spread from the streets to the houses. The Lithuanian Elite Guard, with the help of Polish and Lithuanian youngsters, raided homes and sought out hidden Jews. Hundreds of men were seized daily for transport to Ponary.

Jews were ordered to wear the Shield of David patch. Then came a series of prohibitions: Jews were forbidden to have radios, to use public means of transportation, to sell their belongings, to buy in the public market except at specified times, to speak to non-Jews, to be on the streets after 6 P.M., to appear on the main streets of the city, and to walk two abreast.

On July 4, 1941, two armed Germans came to the main synagogue and demanded to see the chief rabbi of Vilna. The beadle, Chaim Meyer Gordon, told them that one chief rabbi was in America and that the other was dead. "Then you're the rabbi," he was told. He was ordered to see that a representative body of Jews was organized. The beadle, after consulting with Rabbi Samuel Fried, went to the former secretary of the Kehillah, Israel

Werblinski. After several private consultations, he in turn called a meeting of the most prominent leaders in all walks of Jewish life.

At once a debate arose in every organized group—whether to attend or to boycott the meeting. No one had any illusions about what the Germans wanted. Two years of brutal German rule in Poland and the horror stories of the refugees had dissipated any illusions the Jews may have had about self-government. The Germans wanted a Judenrat that would be a body to execute German orders, to make it easier for them to despoil and maltreat the despised subhumans. The only question in the minds of the organizations was whether such a body could also alleviate the coming heavy tribulations of the Jewish community. At last, after many discussions, the meeting was held to elect a Judenrat. A number of nominees refused to serve. The ten finally chosen were a rabbi (representing the religious Jews), a leader of the craftsmen, Abraham Zeidshnur (for the merchants), a lawyer (for the labor intelligentsia), Saul Trotsky (for the industrialists), Anatol Fryd (a banker, head of the Communal Savings Bank), two physicians, a General Zionist, and an engineer. The chairman was Saul Trotsky, vice-chairman was Anatol Fryd, and the secretary was Abraham Zeidshnur. The Judenrat was placed under the supervision of the Lithuanian Authority over Jewish Affairs in the person of Petras Buragas.

The Judenrat was immediately besieged by women wanting to know what had become of their husbands and by Jews driven out of their homes in various quarters of the city. The homeless Jews were billeted with other families, but the Judenrat got no answer to its inquiries about the arrested men. Meanwhile snatching went on. The Judenrat got permission to have 30 to 50 men available in the Judenrat building every night as a reserve in case men were needed for emergency labor; they hoped by that to forestall the night raids that caused such terror. They also came to an agreement with the Elite Guard to supply 150 men but had to back down when only 21 offered themselves as recruits. Snatching was profitable as a source of free labor, and it increased. Germans grabbed men for work in the city, and none returned home; the Elite Guard seized others and few came back. German and Lithuanian units hijacked each other's labor gangs; in the process Jews were the victims. Jewish men disappeared from view to remain in hiding. Families built *malinas* (the word was derived from underworld argot: a *malina* was, in Hebrew, a cache for stolen goods)—cellar bunkers, attic closets, secret rooms, chimney nooks, all sorts of holes where their men would wait out the raids of the snatchers.

Along with the terror of snatching went outright murder. On July 10, 123 men were seized and shot on Hospital Street on the pretext that a German motorcyclist had been fired on. A few days later the meaning of the buses to the Ponary woods, the prewar picnic and camping grounds for the Vilna populace, became clear. At first the stories that the Germans were using Ponary for mass executions of the men brought from the Lukiszki Prison were not believed; such slaughter was incredible. But then came Gentile eyewitnesses from the neighborhood and finally Jewish escapees from the killing grounds itself. Now the Jews knew for certain that to be arrested meant to be shot. The Judenrat felt it urgent to make greater efforts to stop the snatching.

On July 16 it succeeded in getting permission from the Germans to be the sole supplier of Jewish labor gangs, but the Elite Guard paid no attention to the Judenrat's official status. Snatching went on unabated, to such an extent that the Germans interfered on occasion when they themselves needed more workers. Men began to live day and night in their malinas.

By order of the German authorities, on July 24 the Judenrat was enlarged by adding fourteen new members. They were engineers, lawyers, merchants, intellectuals, independent and Labor Zionists, Bundists, a rabbi, and a former vice-mayor of a city near Vilna. The new Judenrat, although more representative of the Jews, was as ineffective as its predecessor in stopping the snatching.

The Germans set up their civilian administrative apparatus for Vilna. On August 1, 1941, Hans Hingst became Regional Commissar and Franz Murer his deputy for Jewish Affairs. Five days later the Judenrat was ordered to "contribute" 5,000,000 rubles to the Germans; otherwise the entire Judenrat would be shot. Two million was to be ready by ten o'clock the following morning. The curfew interfered with the collection so that only 1,490,000 rubles, a half kilogram of gold, and 189 gold watches were ready at that time. Murer relented. His mercy consisted of shooting only two members of the Judenrat and extending the time for the collection. By six that evening another half kilogram of gold, 667,000 more rubles, and 200 additional gold watches were ready for him. The remainder of the "contribution" was made up in the following days.

The Judenrat was ordered to have a specified number of workers available each day. Snatching slowly petered out. It interfered with proper exploitation of Jewish labor needed to work in the many industrial enterprises as well as in menial tasks unfit for "Aryans." The Jews began to breathe more easily; Ponary was fresh in their minds, but they believed that now the blood-lust of the Germans was satisfied. A sad but stable existence seemed to them to be in the offing.

They were mistaken. A group of the Einsatzkommando (Number 3) moved into Vilna. The Einsatzkommandos were special mobile killing units whose mission was to wipe out "Bolsheviks, Jews, and other unreliable elements." Einsatzkommando Number 3, like other German organizations, kept good records. From those records we know that between August 12 and September 1, of 1941, 425 male and 19 female Jews were killed by it in addition to 17 Communists of both sexes. That number, their report reads, did not take into account the approximately 4,000 Jews killed previously.

On September 1, using as an excuse the shooting of a German soldier, the main Jewish section of the city, in its center, was cleared of Jews. The "action" lasted throughout the night and the following day. Old men and women, mothers with children, entire families were driven out, to be taken to Ponary. There 864 male and 2,019 female Jews plus 817 children of both sexes were killed and their bodies thrown into mass graves.

On that same day 16 of the Judenrat members were taken to prison and never again heard of.

Five days later the Jews were suddenly herded into two ghettos.

3

The two ghettos were in the center of the city, the oldest part, picturesque for its narrow cobblestoned streets, tiny alleys, low two-story buildings with wooden doors, many with small shops on the first floor.

The ghettos were set up so suddenly that the Jews expelled from other parts of the city managed, for the most part, to bring with them only the barest necessities of life—pots and pans, bedding, clothes, packages of food. Christian neighbors helped to carry heavy bundles and lent wheelbarrows and pushcarts; other Christians bought cheaply what the Jews had to leave behind; still others waited until the houses were cleared of Jews and then looted the dwellings. The press of people in the ghettos was hardly to be borne; places to sleep were sought and fought over. And yet here, as in Warsaw and in Lodz, many Jews thought the ghettos would be like the medieval ghettos, a place of refuge from the snatchers, a place where Jews could hide themselves from the malignity of the conquerors. The doors of the houses facing the "Aryan" city were nailed shut; each ghetto had a single closely guarded gate. In Ghetto Number One were crowded together 29,000 Jews, in Ghetto Number Two about 11,000.

Not all the Jews obeyed the order to move. Some "passed" as Christians, with the connivance of their Gentile relatives or close friends. Others were hidden, despite the German decree of death for such help, in the houses of Christian neighbors horrified by the reports from Ponary. Still others were given sanctuary for themselves or their children in convents and churches; the Mother Superior of the Benedictine Cloister sheltered, for exampled, leading members of various Zionist Youth organizations. And still others proclaimed themselves Karaites, adherents of a schismatic Jewish sect, of Tartar descent, of whom there were 500

in Vilna, with a synagogue of their own. The Germans hypocriti-
cally said they were not opposed to Judaism as a religion, but to
Jews as a race. They decided that Karaites were "Aryans believing
in Judaism" and hence not subject to the Nazi race laws.

4

The Germans announced that Ghetto Number One was to be
for skilled workmen and their families; Ghetto Number Two was
for the unemployed and for unskilled laborers and their families.
Because of the haste with which the Jews had been shoved into
the ghettos, the discrimination was not exact. In the next few
days, groups and individuals were shuttled from one ghetto to
the other. Those in Ghetto Number Two had no work passes
issued to them. The Jews there knew their days were numbered.
They tried to escape from their assigned ghetto to the supposed
safety of Ghetto Number One.

But Ghetto Number One was no haven. During the night of
September 15, 3,550 Jews were taken to be sent to Ghetto
Number Two. Only 600 arrived there across the intervening
street. The rest were taken to an unknown destination, later
discovered to be the killing ground at Ponary.

More room was made in Ghetto Number Two. On October 1,
800 men were removed in the morning and 900 more at night—to
be killed. Two thousand more were being taken away on October
4, but they rebelled and fought with their bare hands until they
were overcome. Resistance spread, to no avail. On October 16,
3,000 more were removed. Ghetto Number Two was finally
liquidated on October 28 when 2,500 Jews were taken to Ponary.
A few individuals and families succeeded in escaping to Ghetto
Number One. A few more hid in malinas and managed to stay
there for weeks until hunger drove them into the hands of the
searching SS squads.

5

Ghetto Number One was now *the* Vilna Ghetto. On the first

day of its existence, Murer appointed Anatol Fryd as the chairman of a new Judenrat and told him to coopt others, at least four more. Fryd chose the lawyer, Milkanovitsky, an independent Zionist, and the Bundist, Joel Fishman, a skilled shoe worker, both of whom had been in the former Judenrat. He had to persuade Gregory Guchman, an engineer who belonged to no political party, to join because the Judenrat felt the need of an engineer in its councils. The fifth member was the Bundist lawyer, Gregory Jaszunski. Fryd had hidden out in the Jewish Hospital while the mass evacuation and murder of the Jews was going on. There he had met Jacob Gens, acting superintendent of the hospital. Gens, because of his Lithuanian connections and his fearless attitude vis-à-vis the Germans, he nominated to be the chief of the ghetto police. The nomination was approved by the Germans.

6

Jacob Gens was born on April 1, 1903, in Ilgvieciai, a tiny village in the Siauliai district of Lithuania, where his father was a merchant of modest means. Jacob was the oldest of four brothers (another had died in infancy); he had no sisters. Whatever Jewish religious education he had was given at home. He attended a Russian primary school, Lithuanian schools being forbidden by the Tsarist regime. The attempt at forced Russification had no effect on him; he was imbued with love for his native land, an attitude shared by his family. He was then admitted to the *gymnasium* at Siauliai where he stayed two years until his enlistment in 1919 in the new Lithuanian army at the age of sixteen.

Because of his higher education he was immediately sent to Officers' School, from which he was graduated with the rank of junior lieutenant. He saw active service with the army on the Polish-Lithuanian front and from there, still in the army, he was sent to complete his *gymnasium* courses at Marjampole, the most highly regarded institution of its kind in Lithuania. In four months he finished all the required courses (that usually took two years); he passed his examinations with honors. He then returned to his unit, where he was promoted to senior lieutenant. For his active service in the cause of Lithuanian independence he was awarded a military medal.

In 1924, after a courtship of about one year, he married a well-educated young Lithuanian woman of good family (also a recipient of a medal for services to her country) who was employed by the governing body of Ukmerge, a frontier garrison town. At that time Gens applied for transfer from the infantry to the new air force, but the transfer was denied because he was married. He then went into the reserve forces of the Lithuanian army so that he would have time to go to the university at Kaunas. To support himself and his wife he became a teacher.

Lithuanian was the official language of the young republic, but the long period of subjugation to Russia and the rigid restrictions on the use of Lithuanian resulted in a great shortage of teachers of the language. Gens, a graduate of Marjampole, the center of classical Lithuanian education, immediately found work as an instructor of Lithuanian language and literature in a Hebrew high school at Ukmerge; he later took a post in a Yiddish high school at Jurbarkas. In both schools he also taught physical education. His schedule was heavy. Besides teaching he had to commute to Kaunas three times a week for classes. The schools paid his salary irregularly and then the sum was often less than he was supposed to get. His wife, now caring for a daughter (born in 1926), finally convinced him that he must move closer to the university. In 1927 the Gens family moved to Kaunas, where he succeeded in getting a post as chief accountant in the Ministry of Justice. Gens was fluent in Lithuanian, Russian, German, and Yiddish; he also knew Hebrew and had a smattering of Polish and English.

In 1935, after he had received his diplomas in law and economics, opportunities for more gainful employment opened up for him. He left the government job to work for the Shell Oil Corporation in its Kaunas office. He quickly learned the ropes and was recognized as an efficient executive. He worked there for about two years and then took a similar position with Lietukis, the association of Lithuanian cooperatives, a mixed private-state enterprise. Again his competence was recognized. He wrote technical manuals and toured the country giving lectures to consumers' groups on the proper use of gas and oil products. On his tours he often gave anti-Soviet lectures as well.

Gens was a Zionist despite, or perhaps because of, his strong patriotic feeling for Lithuania. He was a Zionist of a special type, a Revisionist, a follower of Vladimir Jabotinsky. Gens was an active member of *Brith ha-Chayal,* a paramilitary organization of Revisionists.

Revisionism, founded in 1925, was regarded by many Jews as the extreme-right lunatic fringe of the Zionist movement. Jabotinsky, a fiery speaker, had long advocated the tearing away of Palestine from the crumbling Ottoman empire by military conquest. The ambiguous Balfour Declaration of 1917, recognizing the claim of the Jewish people to a "national home," accentuated Jabotinsky's impatience with the snail's pace of the world Zionist movement. Now he proclaimed, "We have waited long enough for the ingathering of the exiles—the time has come for us to act."

Jabotinsky, exasperated by the slowness of colonization, the Arab riots against the Jews in 1920 and 1929, and the stupidities of the British pro-Arab and anti-Jewish imperialist rule, advocated radical measures. Immigration to Palestine must be speeded up regardless of Great Britain's regulations. What was illegal to the British was simple justice to the Jews. Jews must quickly form a majority of the population. Everything must be secondary to the building up of Palestine as a Jewish state. To that end, Jews must not employ Arabs but must themselves be the builders and laborers; to encourage the flow of private capital Jews must not be paid more than the native population. Neither religious views (Jabotinsky felt that the Jews were a dispersed nation, not a religious cult) nor socialist ideals were to get in the way of the all-important purpose of Zionism—a homeland for the Jews. He was opposed to labor unions ("Jews are Jews, not capitalists and workers"). He said the time for passivity in the face of attack was past; now self-defense and counter-action were needed. Jabotinsky attracted to his party large numbers of young people, who became organized in groups called *Betarim*. The Betarim put emphasis on physical fitness for agricultural work and military training. They were even more impatient than their leader. They attacked other Zionists, verbally and physically, as betrayers of the cause.

In 1938, as official anti-Semitism rose in Europe, Jabotinsky was pushing for the speedy removal of the Jews of Central and Eastern Europe to Palestine. The Polish government was interested in his plan to evacuate 1,500,000 Jews and was to make representations to Great Britain for implementation of the plan. The Zionist movement, indeed most of world Jewry, was horrified by the proposal. It smacked to them of playing into the hands of the anti-Semites with their slogan of "Jews, get out! Back to Palestine!" The beginning of World War II put an end to the discussion.

In the late thirties Gens was called back from the reserves and sent to Staff Officers' School in anticipation of the need for command officers if war should break out. Because of his brilliance, Gens was known as von Moltke, after the German strategist. He was advanced to the rank of captain and returned to his post with Lietukis.

Two weeks after the proclamation of the Soviet Republic of Lithuania, Gens was summarily dismissed from his position. He discovered that no work permit was to be issued to him nor would he be allowed to reside in Kaunas. Bank accounts being frozen, he was faced with the problem of supporting his family. His brother, Solomon, who had been employed in the Kaunas Bank of Lithuania, had been living since 1939 with his wife and mother in Vilna, where he had been transferred when Vilna became the capital city. Gens went to Vilna, hoping that his dossier would not follow him. He found to his dismay that he was as much persona non grata in Vilna as in Kaunas. Not only was he deprived of the chance of making a living but he was also probably on the list of proscribed persons to be sent to Soviet labor camps. Fortunately he found succor through an old comrade-in-arms, a Colonel Usas, a medical officer who was now head of the health department in Vilna. Colonel Usas put him to work as a book-keeper in that department on a daily basis, a device which kept Gens's name off the official payrolls and which did not require reporting his employment to the political commissar attached to the hospital. Gens lived, unregistered, with his brother and mother. During the mass deportation of "unreliable elements" by the Soviet regime, which began in June, 1941, he slept in the Municipal Hospital so that he would not endanger his brother or mother were he to be arrested.

After the invasion of Lithuania by the Germans, the new rulers ordered all Jews removed from positions in state institutions. Colonel Usas kept Gens in his department, however, until the situation became too dangerous. He then appointed him as director of the Jewish Hospital, then still under jurisdiction of the health department.

The Jewish Hospital was a relatively safe haven during the early period of the German occupation. To its safety fled a number of Jewish notables feigning sickness. Gens made a good impression on them because of the disciplined way he ran the institution in a time of crisis. They also took note of his lack of fear when he spoke to the German officials, before whom most Jews trembled, with good reason.

Gens knew through his Lithuanian army connections, especially through Major Buragas, in the Department of Jewish Affairs, that a ghetto was soon to be formed. At that time his wife and daughter had followed him to Vilna and were living with his brother and mother. On the pretext of appealing to the Lithuanian puppet-premier for protection because of their honored services, Gens sent his wife to Kaunas while he made arrangements for an apartment not too far from the ghetto. When the ghetto was formed, his wife and daughter lived only a short distance away, under his wife's maiden name. They frequently entered the ghetto, mostly during the "actions" in the city, when Gens would be able to guard them. It was rumored that the Gens couple had gone through a *pro forma* divorce; that was not true, although

Gens never denied the rumors, which he felt gave further protection for his family.

Mrs. Gens was opposed to his taking any conspicuous part in Jewish affairs. She said he should merge with the masses, be colorless, even "pass," but Gens replied, "It is not my nature to sit hidden behind a farmhouse oven and fear every bark of a dog." Indeed, he could have "passed." He was tall, with hazel eyes, light brown hair, and an "Aryan" visage. He had good connections with Lithuanians holding office under the Germans. Yet he undertook being police chief because, as he told his wife, "I hope you understand that I cannot abandon the ghetto at a time when my people are suffering so much. I must stay and try to do the best I can for the Jews of the ghetto." He said he expected the job to be unpleasant, one which would give him extensive administrative powers. His wife says he never expected to act the role of a god with power over human lives.

7

The Germans assumed that the Judenrat, aware of the slaughter at Ponary, would be terrified and passively subservient. Terrified and subservient it was indeed, but its members, men of principle, did not forget their responsibility to the Jews of the ghetto. They did not believe, as did Czerniakow in Warsaw, that the Germans merely wanted to squeeze money out of the Jews and would go to any lengths in that process, nor did they think, as Rumkowski did in Lodz, that the Jews could ingratiate themselves with the conquerors by being good and faithful slaves working for the Wehrmacht. Every one of them knew that to the Germans a Jew was not a human being but a kind of noxious animal whose labor could be used until the time came for his extermination. The self-imposed task of the Judenrat was to delay that time for as long as possible.

To that end, in the earliest days of the ghetto, it instituted a series of measures to preserve and maintain the ghetto. The Gestapo had threatened that it would tolerate no epidemics; if any infectious disease appeared, it would liquidate first the hospital and then the entire ghetto. Under the direction of the Judenrat a health department was immediately organized, utilizing a devoted corps of physicians, nurses, and sanitary inspectors. The sanitation division set up baths and disinfection centers, gave popular lectures on the prevention of disease, checked individuals for lice and homes for bedbugs, and started laundries and barber shops. Considering the press in the crowded quarters (200 to 500 persons in a building where previously only 30 to 40 resided), the dark, outdoor privies, water pipes frozen and burst, and the early shortage of food, the accomplishments of the sanitary corps were amazing. The streets and the houses of the ghetto were spot- lessly clean. Attendance at the baths was compulsory; no rations were given out unless the food card had been stamped by the bath attendants. Unlike Warsaw, bribery and evasion of the sani- tary code were nonexistent. The police rigorously enforced every health department regulation.

When the Germans inspected the hospital, they said they were satisfied with it, but they issued a warning that if typhus or other contagious diseases were to appear, they would burn down the hospital with all the patients in it, possibly even the entire ghetto. A few cases of typhus, typhoid, and dysentery occurred during the early weeks of the ghetto; the hospital doctors treated such cases under false diagnoses.

The Germans issued a pharaonic decree: no Jewish women were to bear children. The doctors did abortions on demand, but for those women who wanted to be mothers they set up a special unit for deliveries in the hospital. The infants were not discharged until they looked old enough to be given fictitious certificates of birth antedating the decree. The maternity section was an open secret in the ghetto, yet throughout its entire existence no informer ever told the Germans about it.

The press of living in such crowded quarters and the terror of being subject to German rule frayed the tempers of the ghetto inhabitants. The police kept strict order. Gens ran the police department under rigid discipline, demanding and getting obedience. He recruited strong young men, preferably Betarim (Young Revisionists) whom he could trust. He divided the ghetto into four precincts, each headed by a deputy chief. One was Joseph Muszkat, a lawyer from Warsaw, a Revisionist; he it was who later organized children into a brigade that helped the underground resistance. Another deputy was Salek Dessler, an arrogant, rich young man who was rumored to have Gestapo connections. Oberhart, another deputy, a Viennese Jew, was also thought of as a low character. In contrast, the deputy Joseph Glazman, the former editor of a Revisionist newspaper, was highly esteemed as an honest and honorable man. Gens appointed Mayer Levas to be head of the guards at the ghetto gate; he was regarded in the ghetto as an out-and-out sadist, beating and kicking those unfortunates who incurred his displeasure. The people of the ghetto did not know that his violence was a cover-up for activities necessary and worthwhile for them.

Gens built around himself a strong apparatus, well fed and well housed. To the Betarim core were added others who joined out of the desire for the privileges of a policeman or out of a sense of communal responsibility. The 200 policemen strutted about in semimilitary uniforms ornamented by blue bands and a leather belt, wearing the signs of their rank on their hats and the Shield of David on their arms. They used their authority to the utmost: they cursed, they beat, they made arrests. They swaggered and they shouted, but they did maintain order. At no time was crime a problem in the ghetto, as it was in Lodz. The ghetto Jews shrugged their shoulders and said, "We need them. Better them than anti-Semites." Not until Yom Kippur (October 1, in 1941) did the Jewish populace begin to distrust the police.

On that day, the holiest day of the year for Jews, the Germans decided they wanted more Jews for killing than the hundreds they were collecting from the second ghetto. They demanded at least a thousand more Jews from the main ghetto. German and Lithuanian units invaded the ghetto and started snatching. Gens was fearful that the snatching would end in a general massacre. He persuaded Schweinenberg, the Gestapo officer in charge of the "action," to let the Jewish police do the job. Gens called a meeting of the police force and gave instructions. The police ran around the ghetto calling on all those with white work certificates issued by the Labor Office to go to the gate to have them stamped for further legitimization. There at the gate the hapless Jews, 2,200 of them, were removed to prison by the Germans. Prison, of course, was only a way station to Ponary. Some people looked on the policemen's fatal subterfuge as Gens's work. Others said he meant well but his policemen were over-zealous.

On orders of the Germans Gens made a census of the ghetto, registering all inhabitants by age, sex, and occupation. On October 22, his police helped to remove eight aged and paralyzed Jews to the prison. The Jews shivered in fear of what was to come.

Jewish labor was essential for the functioning of Vilna industry. The Germans announced to the city that Jewish labor was available at a fixed wage through the German Labor Office. It authorized the Judenrat to tax the Jews 10 percent of their wages for administrative needs, warning at the same time that no extensive apparatus was to be set up. The Jews allowed to work outside the ghetto had to go to their jobs in groups by the shortest route and had to return to the ghetto by twilight. To control the labor supply, the Germans voided all white certificates and issued yellow ones, 3,000 altogether, to be distributed to skilled workers by the Judenrat. The yellow certificates were a safe-warrant for the families of the workers as well as for the breadwinners themselves. The families were issued blue cardboard tickets. No more than four persons were counted as a family: man, wife, and two children.

More than the allotted number of 3,000 skilled workers lived in the ghetto. Panic spread like a forest fire. Yellow certificates became an object of trade: ten gold rubles for a certificate. Girls with yellow certificates were lucky; they had a dowry worth more than money. A love song had the line, "I'll watch over you like my yellow pass." Another said, "If you had a yellow pass, I'd marry you right now." Forged certificates appeared at a cost approaching that of the real article. Unmarried women signed themselves as paper wives to single men with yellow certificates. Families with more than two children scrambled from house to house seeking a childless couple or one with an only child so that their "superfluous" children could be adopted pro tem. Widows with unmarried sons painted their faces to look younger so that they would look like wives.

The reason for the yellow certificates was obvious to all—another purge of unemployed workers and their families. The Jews had not long to wait. Starting on October 25 and lasting to November 5, 1941, all Jews found without the yellow certificates were taken to prison and thence to Ponary. Hundreds hid in their malinas, from time to time creeping out in risk of their lives for food and water. The malinas were no surety of safety. The police made searches and uncovered many of them when they heard a suspicious noise or the whimper of a child. Dozens were dragged out daily from the malinas to be added to the hundreds gathered at the gate for removal. The largest haul was on November 3, when 1,200 were seized for extermination. By the time the "days of the yellow certificates" had passed, 8,000 Jews had been slaughtered.

Gens took part throughout in the round-up. He stood at the gate and supervised the removal of Jews without certificates. He seemed on the surface to be a willing and efficient tool of the German authorities in their savagery; yet he tried when he could to turn it aside. For example: One day he stood before the little yard of the Judenrat building, surrounded by Jewish police and in the presence of SS officers. Before him paraded single file the workers holding the yellow certificates, leading their families to be "legitimized." His countenance cold and impassive, he counted off with a cane in his hand, "Father, mother, child, child," and sent the group into the yard for their blue tickets. A family of five appeared. Gens counted to four, thrust aside the last child, a twelve-year-old boy, and struck him with his cane. A murmur of horror went up from the assembled Jews, horror that a Jew should so break up a family and dispose of a child's life. A family of three appeared. Gens counted, "Father, mother, child!" and then shouted, "You blockhead, you! You forgot one child!" The father whispered, head bent, "I have only one child," but Gens paid no attention to the answer and beat him over the head with his cane. During the tumult aroused by his brutality, he grabbed the boy he had thrust aside and put him with the group of three, yelling meanwhile at the man, "You idiot! Here's your child! Next time, dope, don't lose him!"

Gens's police imitated the zeal he showed before the Germans. Sometimes they went too far, Gens let it be known. On one occasion, a policeman accused Gens in Polish in front of a Gestapo officer that Gens was not acting on the information he had been given about a large malina. "You are a dog!" Gens roared and shot him on the spot. The Gestapo officer applauded what he thought was Gens's reply to an act of insubordination.

The police adored Gens and followed his orders no matter how their own lives were endangered by so doing. Bagranski, the director of the Labor Office, decided to try to pass as an "Aryan" with false papers. He was recognized in the city as a Jew and was brought to Gestapo headquarters. There he covertly pushed the documents he had with him behind a radiator. Among them was an address book with names and addresses of Christians in Vilna who hid Jews and helped them to escape from the Germans. It also contained Mrs. Gens's address. Gens feared for his daughter's safety. Policemen volunteered to help. A squad, using the excuse of checking on how well the Jewish charwomen were doing their job, went to Gestapo headquarters and managed to find and remove the documents. Bagranski was later freed, after Gens's intervention and the payment of a large bribe.

But such good deeds were not public knowledge. The Jews could only judge from what they saw and felt. The police were hated and the chief of police hated most. Gens knew of his bad reputation. A delegation of four rabbis came to him to protest his participation in the selections for Ponary. They said that according to Jewish law a Jew could be given up to the governing authority only if he were personally guilty of a crime and not merely because he was a Jew. They told Gens he had no right to turn Jews over to the Germans. Gens replied that by taking part in the selections and surrendering a few Jews, he saved the rest. The rabbis reminded him of the opinion of Maimonides: even if only a single Jew was demanded to be killed, then all should be killed rather than give him up. Gens smiled cynically and dismissed the rabbis.

Still, he tried to justify himself. In a private conversation he said, "People accuse me of being a drunkard and carouser. Right over there stands the very glass from which I just drank wine with the Gestapo bunch, but thanks to the drink I succeeded in rescuing Bagranski from death. Are you judging me that I carry on and get drunk? I stand and count off at the gate, but do you know how hard that is for me? People ask me where they're going and I don't tell them because I know where they're going. I want to save a few, and if possible the best, the most useful, so that they can renew our people."

The Germans appreciated Gens's efforts. His erect, soldierly stance, his air of command, his prompt execution of orders put him on good terms with Murer. The Germans called him "the proud Jew." They gave him a great deal of freedom, trusting him to enforce their decrees against smuggling and sabotage. For that reason they placed no German guards at the ghetto gate. The Lithuanian guards there feared Gens as a Lithuanian army officer and always saluted him smartly when he went through. He got special privileges: he could enter and leave the ghetto at will; he was exempt from the wearing of the yellow badge; the back door of his house, facing an "Aryan" street, was opened. Concomitant with his friendship with the Germans grew his power in the ghetto, even over his technical superiors, the Judenrat.

When "the days of the yellow certificates" were past, the ghetto had two classes of inhabitants: those with certificates and those without. New rules were promulgated: the blue tickets were declared worthless; when the workers were not at home, copies of the yellow certificates had to be left with their families, copies legitimized by the Jewish police. Later pink certificates were issued to persons needed for the ghetto administration. Then, as a result of Gens's intervention with the Germans and as a recompense for the good work he had done, the number of pink certificates was increased. Skilled workers with invalid white certificates could now be given pink certificates giving them the right to work within the ghetto and thus *Lebensrecht,* the right to live. The ghetto police were in charge of registration. So distrustful of the Jewish police were the workers that many of them gave false names and addresses when they signed up. Gens monopolized the issuance of the certificates. He began to put into practice his theory of how to save the Jewish people. He issued the certificates by preference to strong, able-bodied young men and to women of child-bearing age. In them he saw the future, not in the flabby intellectuals and the impractical religious sages. He was not entirely hardhearted, however; he let himself be prevailed on to register under fictitious trades a number of the intelligentsia: writers, artists, even some rabbis. He said it was moral torture for him to decide who was to live under the protection of a certificate and who was to die, but he had no choice.

To the Germans he presented the image of a good and faithful servant. He issued order after order applying the sanctions of fines, imprisonment, or expulsion from the ghetto (meaning death) for evading the wearing of the yellow badge, for leaving the ghetto on private business, for congregating in the streets. The Germans asked for furs. On December 1 the police started a campaign for the "voluntary" surrender of all fur materials and made house searches for hidden furs. Gens commanded those Jews who had left furs outside the ghetto to turn in the addresses where they could be found so that the furs could be handed over to the Germans. A joke spread throughout the ghetto: "When is a goose not a goose [a pun on Gens's name]?" "When he is a fascist parrot." Gens strengthened his hold on the Jews by requiring them to live only in the houses assigned to them; he thus compiled a complete list of names and addresses, making it easier for the police to call on ghetto inhabitants for work assignments—or arrest.

The Germans praised Gens—and kept right on with the extermination. On December 5, 60 men known as "the underworld," strong, healthy men, mostly porters and draymen, were carted off to Ponary, but on the way they fought with their Lithuanian escorts and some succeeded in making their way back into the ghetto. On December 15, the Jews living in the block reserved for laborers for the Gestapo, 300 in all, were taken away. The yellow certificates meant nothing, the holders thereof learned. Three hundred of them were removed from the ghetto to Ponary. Fear and dismay gripped the ghetto. Did the Germans no longer value their own safe-warrants?

Gens reassured the Jews. He pointed out that of the approximately 29,000 pushed into the ghetto only 12,000 now remained but these were all workers and their families. He said, and his ever-rational hearers had to agree with him, that now the German blood-lust was satisfied, that the German war economy needed Jewish labor, that now if the Jews worked for the Germans they would be spared, and therefore by proving their industry they could stave off further sanguinary purges. He had a placard put up: "Jews of the ghetto, take notice! Your work will save your lives!" The more skeptical intellectuals did not believe in the work ideology, but what else could they believe in? At least logic was on Gens's side.

Jews without certificates who had been in hiding, Jews who had escaped from Ghetto Number Two, Jews who had fled from the massacres in Byelorussia and the small towns around Vilna appeared out of nowhere to swell the ghetto population by another 7,000 or more. The Judenrat, following Gens's directives, tried to find work for everyone—men, women, children, the aged—so that all would be regarded as necessary for the German economy. Gens said, "We now have 14,000 workers in the ghetto. In the near future we must have 16,000 registered workers. The more we have, the safer we'll all be."

Besides exhortations to work, Gens rigorously put down dissent. On January 5, 1942, he announced, "I jailed two residents for spreading false rumors and creating panic among the people. I hereby give notice that anyone committing similar offenses will be severely punished."

8

Indeed, the work ideology seemed to be effective. The year 1942 was relatively quiet despite the Jews' feeling that they were living over a temporarily inactive volcano. Snatching was a thing of the past. Columns of Jews marched daily out of the ghetto gate to work in factories in the city or in building new railroad lines or in other construction work; each work brigade was supervised by a Jewish foreman. A number of skilled fur workers and their families were moved to work and live in Kailis, the great fur factory. Others were billeted in the Cheap Houses, a housing project on the outskirts of the city near the H.F.K. enterprise, a German concern. Wages were low, with many deductions, but life was apparently guaranteed. New industries arose within the ghetto to make it more self-sufficient as well as to fill orders given by German firms.

Gens encouraged the growth of such internal industry in the hope that the skills of the Jewish workers in metal fabricating plants, furniture factories, electrical and motor manufacturing would redound to the credit of the ghetto and prove its worth to the Germans. The Germans praised him highly for his initiative in anticipating their needs. At the same time, however, Gens knew of and did nothing to interfere in those same factories with the making of weapons for resistance. For example, he blinked at the kitchenware plant's manufacturing of knives, grenades, and other war material to be smuggled out of the ghetto to the partisans in the nearby woods.

In line with their policy of *Vernichtung durch Arbeit,* meaning extermination through work without enough food to support life, the Germans provided the ghetto with barely enough food for the minimal nutrition of the 12,000 registered workers and their families. But almost 20,000 persons lived in the ghetto. The Judenrat solved the problem of distribution by issuing ration cards, but the problem of provision was beyond its control. No pretense was made about equality of rationing. To the basic uniform ration were added from time to time supplements of bread, flour, sugar, and horsemeat, as these foods were made available. Gens and his staff got two and a half times the supplement, the Judenrat twice the supplement, its officials and other communal leaders less, and so forth down to one eighth for the lowest class, the unemployed. Gens himself saw to it that the intelligentsia received special supplements.

Malnutrition appeared, and some cases of hunger edema and avitaminosis, but only in the very first period of the ghetto. There were no outright deaths from starvation as in Warsaw and no upsurge in tuberculosis as in Lodz. As a matter of fact, the health of the ghetto was fantastically good. The youth and good physical condition of the Jews left in the ghetto, and the rigid enforcement of the sanitary code by the police and the wide range of public health measures, also ultimately under police jurisdiction, kept sickness to a minimum. Jews could not buy medications; doctors permitted to treat "Aryans" wrote prescriptions for fictitious patients. Those medical personnel assigned to work in the city hospital, the military hospitals, and the convalescent home for the Nazi Spanish Battalion "liberated" instruments and drugs. Later, sterilizing equipment was made and drugs synthesized in ghetto factories. Gens cooperated fully with the health department, even to the extent of ordering his police to arrest anyone who looked dirty or whose home was dirty.

The food problem was solved by smuggling, nonexistent in Lodz and difficult in Warsaw. In Vilna smuggling took various forms. The closed wooden doors of houses at the edge of the ghetto opened surreptitiously to admit food products to be bartered for valuables or goods. Through the gate itself food was brought in by workers returning from their jobs in the city. The Lithuanian guards were bribable, the Jewish police cooperative. Only when Germans appeared were the police diligent in their search for contraband brought in by the work brigades. Gens and Levas, the commander of the Jewish gate guards, connived at a ruse to demonstrate how zealous and efficient were the Jewish guards. As the workers came through the gate, some would be stopped by prearrangement (sometimes every third worker, sometimes every seventh, and so on, apparently at random). Their smuggled goods would be taken away and they would be beaten by Levas. Levas was looked on as an insane sadist because there seemed to be no reason why one worker should be beaten for bringing in extra potatoes and one not (a song was written about the apparent senselessness of his actions). Levas knew how hateful he was to the ghetto Jews, but under Gens's influence he consoled himself that he was actually performing a *mitzvah,* a good deed. Unfortunately Levas was caught by Murer one night permitting food trucks to pass through the gate. Even under torture by the Gestapo, Levas did not inform on who had arranged for the food deliveries.

The workers in the brigades all became smugglers. Christians learned to bring food products to the Jewish work places outside the ghetto; there they exchanged the food for clothes, jewelry, cash, and later for goods manufactured in the ghetto. The Judenrat cooperated by buying up smuggled flour, vegetables, and fats from the brigade workers. The Judenrat also hired farmers with carts from the surrounding countryside to remove the ghetto garbage to feed their swine—and expected the farmers to bring in produce.

The Judenrat and the semiofficial Communal Aid Committee joined in trying to see that every individual in the ghetto had enough food. Soup kitchens gave hot meals to the unemployed and the schoolchildren; kitchens supported by the Orthodox Jews, the Bund, and the police gave meals to their clienteles.

Six large bakeries and twenty-eight small ones operated to bake bread from the smuggled flour or from the flour ground from raw grain in the one secret mill still in the ghetto. The price of bread depended on how much flour could be smuggled in. The bakeries also baked bread for individuals from their own flour at the rate of a kilogram of bread for every kilogram of flour. The surplus went to the free kitchens. One of the ghetto chemists was very ingenious: he devised a method of using inedible frozen potatoes to make a sugar syrup out of the potato starch; the syrup was cheap enough to be widely used. Vilna never experienced the famine of Warsaw or the gnawing hunger of Lodz.

Gens knew smuggling was a necessity, but some aspects of it aroused his anger. In a speech to brigade foremen he complained about the commercial transactions being carried on in the factories outside the ghetto. "Who suffer from that? Me. My prestige is lowered, and my prestige is the symbol of the ghetto, of the ghetto Jews. . . . [Were the smugglers arrested] because they tried to save themselves by bringing in a kilo of bread for their wives or children? No. Those six men had to be punished as wrongdoers. On those six men were found not more and not less than 23 bottles of liquor and 20,000 cigarettes. What does this mean to them? That the ghetto swills liquor and smokes the best cigarettes. Doesn't this disturb the ghetto? Isn't this a slap in the face to me, the representative of the ghetto, who's constantly crying to Them about the bad situation of the inhabitants of the ghetto? Who suffers from this? Me and the masses of the ghetto, the poor slobs who bring in piddling amounts for their families. . . ."

Gens persuaded the Germans to allow the brigade workers to bring in a limited supply of food they bought for their own money in the city. He set the amount at five kilograms of potatoes, three kilograms of bread, a bottle of milk, even some butter if the package was not conspicuous. He prohibited the importation of brandy.

The winters at Vilna are cold. Heating material was in such short supply that deteriorated buildings were torn apart by hand for their lumber. Gens got permission for Jews to go out in groups to the nearby woods to chop wood for the ghetto. The woodcutters not only carried in wood but made contacts with the partisans and smuggled in food they had bartered for from the peasants.

Besides the body, the soul of the ghetto had to be maintained. A few days after the ghetto had been established, when all was still in a state of flux and death stood ever-waiting, a delegation of school teachers went to Gens to ask permission to set up an educational system for the children. Gens, who had more vital matters on his mind at the time than education, said impatiently, "Why do you bother me with this? Here, take several buildings and do with the children what you wish." Later, when the killings had ceased, he took a more active interest in the schools, making sure that his appointees served on the curriculum committee so that his Revisionist views would have effect. The Bund, violently opposed to Hebraization and religion in the schools, started a *Kulturkampf* but was defeated. Yiddish was the primary language, but Hebrew and Bible began to be taught in the second grade.

The Bund was also defeated in another campaign against Gens. Life in the ghetto was hard and the future clouded. By Gens's direction the police organized a theater ensemble and provided balls, dances, and other entertainment for the masses to help dispel the gloom of the memory of Ponary and to raise the general morale. Unlike Rumkowski in Lodz, Gens did not censor the songs or productions, although they dealt with the bitterness of ghetto existence and their jokes were often gallows-humor. The Bund put up posters: "One doesn't start theaters in a cemetery!" and "One doesn't go dancing in a graveyard!" The masses paid little attention to the posters. Groups other than the police also organized their own lectures, symposia, choruses, and dance groups.

Gens was annoyed by the posters. He called in Herman Kruk, a prominent Bundist whom he had recommended to the Germans as a learned man to be in charge of the collection of Hebrew and Yiddish memorabilia for the use of the Alfred Rosenberg Institute to Investigate Judaism. He asked Kruk who had put up the posters. Kruk replied, "If I knew, I wouldn't tell you, and if I don't know, why ask me?" Gens said, "Listen, up to now I blinked at your political activities. Now that's over. An end to these games." Kruk answered with the smugness of a True Believer, "Politics is something that comes in through closed doors and windows. Politics is bread. Captains bigger than you fought against politics and went under. Do you think that here in the ghetto you'll do better?" In spite of the insolent response, Gens was polite when he dismissed Kruk. Two days later, however, he issued a warning that those who put up unauthorized posters and placards would be sent to prison. He kept his anger under control; unlike Rumkowski, who used any excuse to get rid of "troublemakers," when the Germans asked him for a list of Bundists and Communists in the ghetto, he told them he knew of none. He also told them that only foolish children talked about resistance, that no partisans had connections with the ghetto, that all the ghetto Jews were solid workers.

To encourage the writers in the ghetto, Gens set up a Vilna Publishing House, as well as a ghetto wall newspaper of six to twelve pages for announcements and news. He gave honoraria to writers on the completion of works, and prizes in various fields of literature. He attended literary gatherings and often used the occasion, as Rumkowski did, to justify himself. At one meeting, for instance, where prizes were awarded to a novelist and a poetess, he said,

Many Jews regard me as a traitor and many of you wonder why I show myself at this literary gathering. I, Gens, lead you to death and I, Gens, want to rescue Jews from death. I, Gens, order the uncovering of malinas and I, Gens, try to get more food and more work and more certificates for the ghetto. I cast my accounts with Jewish blood and not with Jewish respect. If they ask me for a thousand Jews, I give them because if the Germans themselves came, they would take with violence not a thousand but thousands and thousands and the whole ghetto would be finished. With a hundred I save a thousand; with a thousand I save ten thousand. You're people of spirituality and letters. You keep away from such dirty doings in our ghetto. You'll go out clean. And if you'll survive the ghetto, you'll say, 'We came out with a clear conscience,' but I, Jacob Gens, if I survive, I'll go out covered with filth and blood will run from my hands. Nevertheless, I'd be willing to stand at the bar of judgment before Jews. I'd say I did everything to rescue as many Jews as I could and I tried to lead them to freedom. And in order to save even a small part of the Jewish people, I alone had to lead others to their deaths. And in order to ensure that you go out with clear consciences I have to forget mine and wallow in filth.

Political parties other than the Bund took on new life, their activities culminating on January 23, 1942, in the formation of the United Partisan Organization, a disciplined resistance group.

Religious circles were few, but a seminary was started with thirty students who worked by day and studied at night. Muszkat, one of the police precinct captains, organized the orphaned children to work at carrying brick for construction and shortened the work day for them so they could attend school later. Books were contributed and a library set up, with over 300 books being lent out daily.

The ghetto was a city in minature and, despite the widespread communal institutions and the strength of the socialist parties who demanded, "One Ghetto, One Class," class distinctions remained as in any city. When they were driven into the ghetto, most Jews did not bring in more than the permitted 300 rubles, but the more venturesome concealed in their packs and valises all sorts of jewelry and other valuables, which gave them an advantage in bartering. Some Jews were lucky in that the dwellings to which they were assigned by pure chance were homes where wealthy merchants had lived. There they found potatoes and food in the cupboards, pots and pans, extra bedding, chinaware and art work, sometimes even gold in hidden safes. The smugglers and the draymen, the latter because of the facility with which they made outside contacts, were as well off as the factory managers and bosses. The ghetto police were in the same category as the smugglers. Chimney sweeping was traditionally a Jewish occupation in Vilna; the chimney sweeps had special passes allowing them to leave the ghetto at will. They became an avenue of communication between the ghetto dwellers and the "Aryan" citizens of Vilna; they also became part of the upper stratum of ghetto society.

Gens took a hand in every activity, even in the resistance movement. He knew, for instance, that his deputy, Joseph Glazman, was vice-commander of the United Partisan Organization. As long as nothing was done to arouse German counteraction, he did not interfere with the underground organization. He took over the Labor Office and demonstrated his power by issuing more work certificates. He controlled the Housing Office, which registered occupants, applied sanctions for violations of the sanitary code, and mediated between tenants in their quarrels. The Judenrat sank quickly into a secondary role alongside Gens and said openly that Gens was the real ruler of the ghetto.

Gens did not ignore the Judenrat. He saw that the taxes levied by it were collected. Its Welfare Department got money from the *valuta* discovered by his police. He promoted voluntary contributions from the luxury restaurants; from time to time he levied extraordinary taxes on the upper class, especially on the chimney sweeps. He encouraged the turning over of "liberated" goods to the Judenrat departments. Informers told the Germans about hidden merchandise; the Germans told Gens; his police made raids. Some of the uncovered goods they took for themselves, some was given to the Judenrat, and only the remainder was turned over to the Germans. The police also arranged for much of the smuggled flour to be sold to the Judenrat and maintained a rigid price control over bread and other foods.

Gens had one unusual way of getting money for the Judenrat treasury. With the German invasion many Jews hid pots of Russian gold coins in their gardens or backyards. Any treasure so buried was lost if it was outside the ghetto. Gens let it be known that he would pay for information about such gold. He then got permission from the Germans to send selected workers to the hiding place to dig up the pots. Half went to the Gestapo and half to the Judenrat. In that way he accomplished two things: replenishing the communal funds so that more smuggled food could be paid for and raising of his esteem in the eyes of the Germans as a trusted collaborator.

9

The fiction of Judenrat government was ended on April 22, 1942. Murer issued orders that (1) Police Chief Gens was given full responsibility for the ghetto; (2) his police were to maintain order in the ghetto, execute directives of the regional commissar, and see that the work brigades marched off in columns; (3) the watchmen at the gate were not to allow the importation of food into the ghetto; (4) the police chief was warned that failure to comply with German commands meant his death.

Gens did not hesitate to show his authority. On June 3, the Jewish police hanged six men in the ghetto. Of the six, five had been convicted of murder during the course of a robbery. In his speech at the execution, Gens said, "Only 16,000 Jews are left out of the 75,000 Jews of Vilna. These 16,000 must be good, honest, and diligent in their work. Anyone who isn't awaits the same fate at our hands as these six. . . ." The sixth man, Yankel Avidan, had been convicted of stabbing a Jewish policeman. The latter recovered from his wound, but Gens took this opportunity to get rid of Avidan, a known informer for the Gestapo.

Gens wanted his orders carried out without question. On one occasion he himself struck a doctor who refused to go on a medical team for the peat-cutters. He called a meeting of representatives from various associations which had complained about the inequities in the distribution of the food supplements. The meeting was short. Gens said, "I am the ghetto. I alone am responsible for the ghetto and what goes on in it. Whoever opposes me will be expelled from the ghetto." When others wanted the floor, he shouted, "No discussion! Beat it!" The Bundist leaders, angered by his cavalier attitude, called for a boycott in the form of Coventry for Gens and mass resignations from ghetto offices. Neither took place because Gens won popular support by getting the release of 400 Jews from prison to go as lumber workers in the forest, where some melted away into the ranks of the partisans.

The Judenrat, now literally only an advisory council, was formally dissolved by the Germans on July 10, 1942, on the grounds that it was superfluous, a waste of time in meetings and parliamentary debates. Full power was given to Gens. He appointed Fryd as his administrative deputy and, more or less under duress, Salek Dessler as the new chief of police. Dessler was a precinct police deputy; he was the ne'er-do-well son of a rich Jewish philanthropist, a former student at the University of Vilna, a Revisionist. He was tall, robust, broad-shouldered, domineering and brutal in manner, secure in his position as a Gestapo informer. Gens did not trust Dessler; he warned his wife and daughter to be guarded in their speech when Dessler was present.

Gens issued a proclamation:

> The basis for the existence of the ghetto is work, discipline, law and order. Every resident of the ghetto who is capable of working is one of the pillars on which the ghetto rests. There is no room among us for those who shirk work and who by devious means engage in criminal activity.
>
> Out of conviction that all the residents of the ghetto will understand the spirit of my words, I have decided on the release of all who are in the ghetto jail. I hereby declare a general amnesty. In this way I give the transgressors of yesterday a chance to redeem themselves and to go straight for their own sakes. But let no one think that, in time of need, I shall refrain from taking strong measures against criminal elements.
>
> I hope that all the residents of the ghetto, without exception, will support me.

Memories of Ponary were fading when suddenly the volcano erupted again. On Gens's orders, presumably following those of the Germans, 86 aged Jews were taken away and sent to an unused reformatory in the suburbs of Vilna. News came to the ghetto that the old people were well treated there, but no one trusted the Germans. They had reason for distrust. A short time later the old people were shot. Rumors arose that women and children would go next. Gens denied the rumors, saying that the old men and women were unproductive and a drag on the ghetto, ergo——. To prove his point, a few days later when the Germans demanded 300 Jews for execution because of violation of various German rules, including the smuggling of food, Gens bargained with them and got the number cut down to 80—and all those were elderly persons.

The ghetto became panicky. New malinas were built and old ones enlarged in anticipation of coming actions. Smuggling stopped temporarily. Every German decree was strictly obeyed for fear of a provocation. Gens became something of a hero in the eyes of the people when he vigorously denied a German charge that the hospital lights were being used to signal Soviet planes. Despite the threat that he would be shot for his denial, he stood fast and complained to higher-ups that the German who had threatened him was a disturber of the peace.

He was able to act so courageously because he was on good terms with the Gestapo and the SS command. He gave them bribes, he partied with them, he invited them to ghetto musicales, in every way acting as though he were the ruler of the ghetto on a par with them.

And withal he was forced to announce their murderous edicts. On the eve of Rosh Hashanah (September 17, 1942) a poster was put up over his signature:

> Six Jews ran away from the Bialewaker Camp. The German command ordered 10 Jews shot in the same camp for each runaway; that is, 60 adults, not counting children. The punishment was meted out: 60 adults and 7 children were shot there.
>
> A similar punishment awaits the population of the Vilna Ghetto for a similar occurrence.
>
> I greet all the residents of the ghetto on the New Year. I wish everybody health, tranquillity, and a happy future.

For the High Holy Days he ordered all shops, schools, and institutions to be closed, but the workers on jobs outside the ghetto were not exempted from their labor. On Kol Nidre night (the eve of Yom Kippur) Gens, wearing a prayer shawl, asked to speak as soon as the cantor finished the opening prayer. He said, "Let us start with a Kaddish for those who are gone. We have passed through a hard year. Let us pray to God that the coming year will be easier. We must be calm, disciplined, industrious." The congregation wept at his word. Tears rolled down his cheeks.

He had good reason to weep. His free and easy contacts with the Germans gave him information others did not have. He wanted the Jews to be less conspicuous in the eyes of the Germans. He issued a series of warnings to the work brigades going outside of the ghetto. To the women he said: Go out in sober clothes, don't wear hats, don't use lipstick or powder, don't take off the yellow patch and wander around the streets, don't consort with Germans. To the men he said: Be respectful to all non-Jews, take off your hat and bow when you address a German, report promptly all work accidents, be on time for work because tardiness and absenteeism will be counted as sabotage, the penalty for which is death. For two days he argued with the Gestapo against surrendering ten women food-smugglers on the grounds that he should be permitted to punish the offenders. He lost the argument.

He issued the sumptuary warnings because the Germans spoke freely in his presence about getting rid of the Jews. To them, Jews were nonhumans worthy of their hatred. That hatred they expressed openly. Martin Weiss, the infamous commandant of the slaughter grounds at Ponary, stood at the gate one day and found a man who had hidden in his clothing two potatoes and a piece of salted food. He shouted, "You dog! You can't bring in food!" and shot the man right there. On another occasion he sneered at an overburdened worker, "I've killed your father, mother, and sister. Now I need your labor. Don't worry. Later you'll be killed, too." In turn, the Jews looked on the Germans as wild beasts of the jungle, and as such, by nature inhuman and irrational in their acts, to be avoided as far as possible.

Life went on. Work went on. Children went to school. People ate and drank but were not merry because they felt the chill of tomorrow's death.

The terrible news of the slaughter of the 300,000 Jews of Warsaw filtered into the ghetto. Gens was determined to save the Vilna Ghetto. He pushed for orders from German firms, he set up workshops to make articles of luxury for local German officials, and he agreed to a most shameful act in order to spare the Vilna Ghetto from the fate of Warsaw. In mid-October, 1942, he arranged for the selection for extermination of 400 Jews from the town of Oszmiana, fifty kilometers from Vilna; a task force of the Vilna Jewish police actually made the selections, and seven Jewish policemen with eight Lithuanians carried out the executions.

That ignominious deed shook Gens's prestige in the ghetto. Up to then he had been feared and hated but still thought of as a man who meant well. The massacre at Oszmiana showed the ghetto how indifferent he was to life in the desire to save lives. He tried to justify himself. At a meeting he said he had chosen for death only old men and women who had already had years of life, in order to save women and children. "In the villages of Kimeliszek and Bistritz the Jewish police took no part and the Jews there were slaughtered regardless of age or sex. Only 50 Jews were left in Kimeliszek. I could have saved more. . . Now Jews from other villages come and beg me for help. I could have said I don't want to soil my hands by sending my police to do the dirty work but I feel it's my duty to soil my hands. . . . It's our duty to save the young and the strong and not let ourselves be swayed by sentiment. . . ." He pointed out that of the 400 killed only 18 were men under forty years of age. "I don't know if you've all understood my words and if you'll say I was right after we're freed from the ghetto, but this is the viewpoint of the police—Save! Save what we can and don't reckon our personal

future! I count on your moral support. Even now a lot of Jews
don't understand our great danger, how many times a day we're
in jeopardy of going to Ponary. I want you to understand what
our life is in its entire nakedness. . . . I take on myself responsibility for everything that happened. I don't want any discussion. I
called you together to spell out to you fully why a Jew dips his
hands in blood. . . . True, our hands are covered with our
brothers' blood, but we had to perform this terrible task. We're
clean before history. . . . Who knows if They'll ask for more victims, from here or from there? We'll give them the old and the
sick, no children at all. Children are our hope. So are the young
women. When They asked us for workers [to be deported], I
answered, 'No workers. We need them.' So They went out into
the streets of the city and caught a thousand Poles to be sent to
Riga. Who can guarantee the future? In the future if we have
to repeat what we did we'll do it again. . . ."

The speech had the desired effect on some. One commentator,
by no means friendly to Gens, said, "It is horrible, perhaps the
worst of all predicaments, but still there is no other way. Blessed
be the God of Israel, who sent us this man [Gens]!. . . . The young
[the police] have accepted this dreadful duty. . . . The results:
over 400 souls have perished—elderly people, the weak and sick,
retarded children. However, 1,500 women and children were
saved. If this had been the work of strangers, 2,000 persons would
have died, God forbid."

The rest of 1942 passed quietly. The wheels of industry turned,
1,500 children attended school, sport clubs appeared, cultural life
broadened, theater performances were given almost daily, workers got an increase in wages, provisioning improved. Gens
legalized the clandestine religious schools and changed their
hours so that the children could attend regular school. And in
the midst of the quiet, rumors arose of new purges to come and
Gens denounced the rumor-mongers. He said, stressing the
importance of the ghetto population as a work force, "We have
. . . shown that we are very useful and irreplaceable. Under present war conditions, work in general and work for the German

army in particular is the order of the day. . . . It is urgent that we make changes to increase productivity and thus increase the justification for our existence. . . ." The people listened—and built more malinas.

10

The idea of resistance developed early in the ghetto. On January 1, 1942, the Young Zionists of all factions issued a joint proclamation in Hebrew and Yiddish:

Let Us Not Go Like Sheep to the Slaughter!
Jewish youth, place no confidence in those who lead you to extermination! Of 80,000 Jews in the Jerusalem of Lithuania only 20,000 survive. Our parents, our brothers and our sisters have been torn from us before our eyes.
Where are the hundreds of Jews snatched for work by the kidnappers?
Where are the women and the children who were taken from us during the awful night of the provocation?
Where are the Jews snatched on Yom Kippur?
And where are our brothers from the second ghetto?
Whoever was taken beyond the ghetto gate will never return. All Gestapo roads lead to Ponary, and Ponary is death.
Cast aside your illusions! Your children, wives, and husbands are dead! . . .
Hitler aims to destroy all the Jews of Europe. It is the lot of the Jews of Lithuania to be the first in line.
Let us not go like sheep to the slaughter!
True, we are weak and helpless, but the only answer to the murderers is resistance!
Brothers, better to fall as free fighters than to depend on the mercy of the killers!
Let us fight to our last breath!

The proclamation was the needed spark to light the fire of resistance. On January 23, 1942, over the opposition of some leaders (mainly Bundists) on ideological grounds, the United Partisan Organization was formed. Its primary aim was to organize an armed revolt should the Germans attempt any further mass deportations from the ghetto; it also was to engage in sabotage and eventually to unite with the partisan units in the nearby forests. That union was to take place only if fighting in the ghetto were to end by the destruction of the ghetto buildings. The U.P.O. members were realists. They recognized that an armed conflict with the Germans would be an unequal battle and that escape from the ghetto was virtually impossible for the masses of the Jews, the ghetto not being on the outskirts of the city but in its center. They hoped, however, that a ghetto revolt would initiate a rebellion against the occupying forces by pro-Soviet Lithuanians and by Poles fighting for independence.

For that reason, attempts were made to get support from "non-Aryan" sources. They met with no success. The leaders of the Polish Socialist Party in Vilna asked a messenger from the U.P.O., "How can *you* help *us*? What good will contacts between us be?" The Communist groups in the city were well underground and, although they established relations with the U.P.O., were chary of any proposed combined action. The Communist partisans in the forests were willing to accept individual resistance-fighters into their ranks but only if they brought guns with them.

The U.P.O. was organized in a strict conspiratorial manner as an embryo military unit. Its commander was Itzik Vittenberg, a Communist, and the vice-commanders were Aba Kovner, a member of the Zionist Hashomer Hatzair, and Joseph Glazman, a Revisionist. On the staff were representatives of the General Zionists, the Bund, and a former major in the Polish army, Isidor Frucht.

The U.P.O. began immediately to smuggle weapons, sometimes piecemeal, into the ghetto. A small arsenal was quickly collected: thirty revolvers, five machine guns, fifty grenades, several rifles, and thousand of rounds of ammunition. To these were added the weapons secretly made in the ghetto machine shops, enough to arm every fighter and to have a reserve. To finance its operations, the U.P.O. collected money from sympathetic Jews and sold counterfeit ration cards in the city.

Gens's relationship with the U.P.O. was ambiguous. He knew of its existence. It would have been hard for him not to. Glazman was one of his closest friends and other Revisionist party comrades were in it. But Gens wanted no details and pretended to know nothing about it. He made no attempt to suppress it or other resistance groups. He was on good terms with the Communists. He, like every other Jew, was confident that Hitler would be defeated. He expected the Red Army to return to Vilna. In that case he wanted friends at court. On one occasion when a member of the U.P.O. was arrested in the city for doing business with "Aryans," Vittenberg went to Gens to have him intercede with the Germans for his release. Gens was very cooperative and arranged for the man's being set free.

Other resistance groups also arose, made up mostly of nonpolitical young people. These units eventually came together in a single organization known as "Scheinbaum's group," named after its leader. Scheinbaum believed that resistance inside the ghetto was useless and that the sole hope of the Jews was to gather weapons and escape from the ghetto to join the partisans. Gens did nothing to thwart them as long as they confined themselves to propaganda and training. His aim was to keep order in the ghetto. If Scheinbaum's group caused no trouble, he had no objections to what they did. The Germans were not his friends.

Neither were the Communists when they did what he considered harmful and dangerous for the Jews. At the end of January, 1943, he fined the Left Front (an organization of Communists and fellow-travelers) 10,000 rubles for collecting money for the Soviet prisoners of war quartered in the Cheap Houses. The money was paid over to the Communal Aid Committee, now a welfare organization controlled by the police, the Zionists, and the Orthodox, to the chagrin of its Bundist founders.

Murmurings arose against Gens for his authoritarianism. Gens said they were the work of doctrinaire intellectuals and paid little attention to them. He felt that the masses understood him. He beamed when the children at a public Seder at Passover acted out a new Haggadah (the story of the Exodus) in which he was hailed as a hero in Israel.

He continued his interest in the school program. At a debate on a proposed new curriculum he expressed his opinion that Glazman was correct in his advocacy of a Jewish nationalist approach by teaching the children Hebrew, the geography of Palestine, and Jewish history. At the spring graduating exercises he told the assembled children, "Be comradely, brotherly, obey your parents, love your people, work for the ghetto. Be proud and firm Jewish children."

Over the ghetto hung gathering clouds of doom. The slaughter of Jews in the towns surrounding Vilna went on unabated. Only the strong and healthy Jews were saved to be sent, some to the Kaunas Ghetto and some to the Vilna Ghetto. Gens was worried about the future. He ran to the Regional Commissar, to the Gestapo, to the SS offices, reporting on the unquiet mood of the ghetto and asking whether the Vilna Ghetto was to be liquidated like those of Bialystok and Grodno. The German officials laughed and told him that those other places had been pure ghettos but the Vilna Ghetto was not a ghetto, but rather a giant labor camp whose work was essential to the German war economy. Reassured, Gens repeated to the ghetto masses what he had been told.

He repeated it but was not altogether convinced by it. He wanted to make the Jews less visible in the eyes of the overlords. Again he warned the women about going to work too well dressed, he fulminated against the use of alcohol, he accused "criminals" (those who violated German regulations) of bringing shame to the ghetto, he forbade smoking in public as a sign of luxury. His reassurances and his warnings had their effect. The uneasy mood of the ghetto began to die down.

Not for long. In March of 1943 all certificates were invalidated, arousing fear that the days of the colored passes were to return. Again the fears were allayed. Instead of the certificates, Jews had to carry around their necks at all times leaden dog-tags bearing their registration numbers.

Gens, too, was nervous. He wanted to show the Germans how trustworthy he was. First, he introduced flogging as a punishment. Second, he ordered police raids on private houses to enforce his order that no one was to have more than one kilogram of flour at any time, to preclude the accumulation of large reserves for speculation. Third, he strengthened the watch over places where goods were being smuggled into the ghetto and he forbade the wearing of coats to work outside the ghetto to cut down large-scale smuggling; his orders were meant to forestall any retributions by the Germans for violations of the antismuggling edicts. Fourth, he applied the principle of collective responsibility: the families of "lawbreakers" would be imprisoned together with them. Six men had been seized with contraband; their families (including those not related but registered as family in order to get *Lebensrecht*), a total of fourteen persons, were taken away the same day to be shot by the Gestapo.

Along with the strong hand went soothing words. He tried to explain away the increasing concentration of village Jews in the ghetto by quoting the German decree that no Jew was permitted to live within fifty kilometers of the old Byelorussian border. They would stay in the ghetto only temporarily before they were sent to labor camps. The Jewish police would be in charge of housing them and seeing they got work; he himself would do all in his power to lighten the burden of the displaced Jews.

The explanation sounded reasonable, followed as it soon was by the German order for a reshuffling of population. The provincial Jews in the Vilna Ghetto were to be sent to the Kaunas Ghetto. Those Vilna Jews with relatives in Kaunas and those who wanted to leave Vilna were permitted to go with the transport. Many Jews signed up to go because they had heard life in the Kaunas Ghetto was easier, with better food and housing. A train of eighty cars was scheduled to leave on April 5. Gens and Dessler, a contingent of police, and a medical team would accompany the transported Jews and help them in the resettlement.

But on that morning, when Gens saw that the train was not

on the main track to Kaunas, he got very excited. He began cursing and ran to the train, ordering the police and medical personnel to leave at once and go back to the ghetto. He saw through the Germans' trickery. He was right. The train went to Ponary where, after a brief but violent resistance, the entire transport of 5,000 Jews was shot.

Gens and Dessler stayed secluded in the ghetto for three days while the terrible story of the massacre ran from house to house. Neugebauer, the Gestapo chief, sent for Gens to discuss the action. Told about the horror with which the news had been received, Neugebauer merely waved his hand and said, "You don't have to worry. The Vilna Ghetto is safe."

Gens took the answer as a proof of the need to increase ghetto productivity. He called a meeting of twenty prominent ghetto leaders. There he said frankly that the Germans had deceived him about the Kaunas transport but that maybe they didn't all know about the planned slaughter. Questions were raised about the morality of taking the baggage of the dead Jews for the benefit of the ghetto. Gens answered, "Better us than strangers." He ended his remarks with, "I can't assure you there will be no further actions. An action against nonproductive elements is certainly possible. Therefore, work hard and prove our industriousness."

The ghetto populace kept quiet. Any illusion they might have had that productivity would save them was shattered. The transport had carried not only old and weak but also men and women in the bloom of youth, sturdy and strong, skilled workers. The Germans evidently could get along without Jewish labor. The illusion that Gens could help was gone, too. If he knew in advance what was coming and did not tell the Jews, then he was indeed a villain; if he did not know, he was as helpless, in spite of his position, as other Jews. Those who had clung to the idea that Gens was an honest man doing the best he could, a guardian of the ghetto, began to lose faith in him. A sad play on words was repeated everywhere: *"Iz Gens a fartreter oder a farfirter?"* A traitor or a dupe? Who knew?

The resistance movement was now face to face with the problem of what to do. The U.P.O. code said that those who left the ghetto were deserters in the face of the enemy, but many members felt it was better to live and fight in the forests rather than wait for the final conflict. The unaffiliated Scheinbaum group was the first to send twenty-eight men out secretly to join the partisans. Their departure became widely known. Gens took note of it by criticizing them as cowards who wanted to save their own lives and who left their families behind. He not only criticized; he took action by removing from their posts those administrators he knew favored the Scheinbaum group. Gens's comments now carried little weight with the Resistance. He was looked on as a pawn in the hands of the Germans. Individuals belonging to neither of the two resistance groups began to buy weapons and prepared to fight for their lives.

Signs of the imminent liquidation of the ghetto increased. In the middle of May the doors of the "Aryan" houses bordering the ghetto were walled up and the tenants in them forced to move out. Smuggling became more difficult and escape from the ghetto even more so. The price of weapons bought by the work brigades in the city went up. Gens, fearful that the purchase of arms would bring disaster to the ghetto, called a meeting of the brigade foremen. He said there that the Germans were laughing at the stupidity of the Jews for buying arms, but that Neugebauer had warned him he would stand for no such nonsense and that if the practice went on he would wipe out the ghetto. "Therefore," Gens cautioned, "watch out! Watch what you do and what your neighbor does. If I discover any 'importations' I'll punish the man responsible, the brigade foreman, the family, maybe everyone who lives in the same house or on the same block."

Meanwhile the pace of industry quickened. Gens pleaded with the 5,000 women who were housewives to go to work. New factories producing for the German army opened. The ghetto administrative apparatus was reduced so that more workers could be supplied. Privately owned sewing machines were requisitioned for the workshops. Some factories were so busy that they worked day and night in three shifts. Of the 20,000 Jews in the ghetto, 13,800 were working by July 14. Food supplies were increased. And still more orders came in for military boots, for winter uniforms, for knapsacks.

And still more weapons were smuggled into the ghetto. Gens ordered stricter searches at the ghetto gate. During one such search a young man was found with a revolver. He begged the guard to let him go because he was planning to join the partisans, but the guard refused. Cornered, the young man shot and killed the policeman. He tried to escape but Gens himself pursued him and shot him. At the policeman's funeral, Gens said, "Today I shot a man. A man, not a Jew. A Jew only by the fact of his circumcision but actually an alien. Had he been a real Jew, he would not have done this [the killing of the policeman]. . . . The police will not be deterred from their work for fear they may fall victims in the course of their duty because the ghetto is dear to them. . . . The enemy is not only external, but internal as well. . . ."

Gens armed his police and had them make raids to uncover arms caches, yet his position vis-à-vis the resistance remained equivocal. In one such raid a young man was found who said he was a messenger from the partisans in the forests. Taken to Gens after a severe beating, he told Gens that he had been sent to recruit men for the partisans and he asked that he not be hindered in his mission. After a rigorous cross-examination, Gens felt satisfied that the young man was telling the truth. He tried to reason with him. "How many do you think you'll save by your tactics, 300, 400, 500? Suppose you get 500, don't forget there are 20,000 in the ghetto. If the ghetto was to be liquidated, I'd tell them all to run. But where to?"

"To the forests. They'll know we have a base there."

"Good thinking," Gens answered with a smile. "You'll have a base but not for 20,000. The ghetto is more to me than to you with your infantile dreams. The ghetto is a world alone, a special world. The ghetto is a death chamber which holds men, women, and little children. The death sentence has already been pronounced but not yet carried out, and the final date is not known.

I want to postpone that date, postpone it with all my potential, with all my strength, as much as I can. Let there be a thousand victims, but I'll not permit a general liquidation of the ghetto. Who among you dares to hasten that day of liquidation? Who of you has the right to shorten the days and hours of children and women who live in the ghetto? If the children are fated to live another day, another hour, I'll fight for that hour for them. . . . I'm not armed with ideals like you, I'm not armed by visions of honor and a hero's death in the resistance. . . . I have neither secret nor open help. . . . The only weapon I have is time. I want to avert the end through work. Through work by healthy men. Thanks to that the ghetto exists. I maintain the ghetto by those very people you'd take away. The Germans wouldn't keep a ghetto for women and children very long; they wouldn't give them food for one extra day. I won't let you destroy the foundation of the ghetto, especially now when the military-political situation is getting better, when the Germans are running from the Russian front, when Rommel's being thrown out of Africa, when Italy's regime has changed. Who can tell what's going to be tomorrow morning or evening, or the next day? Throw away your fantasies, your heroism. They're superfluous here. . . . When I ask Lithuanian officers, old comrades of mine, 'How can you shoot unarmed people, women and children?' they answer me, 'We won't shoot you. Nothing will happen to you. We'll rescue you. To us you're not a Jew but a real Lithuanian.' But I don't want anything for myself. I only want that even a few will survive the ghetto, how many I don't know. In any case, more than I hope, more than you're looking for."

Dessler, standing at Gens's side during the speech, nodded and added, "He could have left the ghetto long ago, but he felt a sense of responsibility. He'll stay here until its destruction or its liberation. . . ."

At last Gens let the young man go free, saying, "Go, if that's your mission. If we're going to be allies, then come to our aid." He not only freed the young man but he also allowed him to leave the ghetto next morning under the guise of a work brigade with a group of seventeen men recruited for the forest partisans. The U.P.O. saw in the gesture a possibility that Gens was changing his mind about resistance inside the ghetto.

Sounded out on what he thought about joining the resistance, Gens said frankly, "We are faced with the problem of going to the forest. This is what I think. It would be easy for me to be accepted by the partisans. Although I am not a supporter of Bolshevism, I would be more willingly received than all of you because I am an ex-officer and know how to use weapons. But I don't want to go. . . . Here is the question—one or 20,000? . . . Supposing 500 left. When I think of that, I put myself in Neugebauer's shoes. If I were he, I would liquidate the ghetto in one go, because one would have to be an idiot to let the ghetto become a reserve for the partisans. But Neugebauer is no idiot. He is a smart man. . . . There is my answer—no. . . ."

In spite of Gens's openly expressed negative attitude, the U.P.O. still hoped for his full support.

The Glazman affair showed they were wrong. Joseph Glazman had distinguished himself in the ghetto as a cultural leader with a good reputation. Gens was vexed by the invidious comparisons being made between him and his deputy. He felt that he was unappreciated by the ghetto. Gens, with his respect for history, as was shown by his encouragment of the gathering of archival materials, was bothered by the thought that future generations of Jews would despise him as a bloody villain whereas Glazman would appear as a communal hero. More than once he complained in private conversations that nobody gave him proper credit for what he was doing for the Jews. He was further annoyed by Glazman's favoritism toward Revisionists. Gens had said more than once during his conflict with the Bund that factionalism and party politics had no place in the ghetto, where all Jews had to unite for a single aim—survival. At last he turned openly against Glazman. He dismissed him as deputy chief and gave him the lesser post of housing administrator.

After the executions at Oszmiana which had so embittered the Jews against the police, Gens and Dessler notified Glazman that he was to go to Swenciany, a town near Oszmiana, to reorganize the housing department there. Glazman, convinced that the job was a subterfuge to implicate him in another pending Oszmiana affair, categorically refused to go.

Gens called a meeting of the police force at which he assailed the "stinking intellectuals" who obstructed his work. Of Glazman he said, "I don't consider him such a *Tsaddik* [righteous man]. Only a year ago he was helping me in the selections for deportation. Now all of a sudden he wants to play the role of a saint." On his order Glazman was arrested. Vittenburg and Chiene Borowska (another Communist) went to intercede for Glazman. The Soviet offensive was then at its height and Gens, not wanting to antagonize the Communists, let Glazman go. In the following months Glazman was called in several times for police interrogation on various charges of embezzlement and theft (during the clearing out of Ghetto Number Two he had appropriated goods and valuables which were later bartered for weapons and ammunition), but he was not again arrested.

On July 25, 1943, Glazman was ordered to go with a police escort to Resza, a nearby village, to join a peat-cutting squad. Glazman was suspicious and refused to go. Dessler sent four policemen who handcuffed Glazman and dragged him by force to the police station. The U.P.O. was immediately mobilized for the rescue of its vice-commander. As Glazman, handcuffed and chained to a cart, was being driven to the ghetto gate, the police escort was overpowered. Glazman was freed and taken in triumph to U.P.O. headquarters.

Crowds filled the streets, cheering the brave young men who had bested the police. Gens, who had been out of the ghetto at the time, arrived a few minutes later. He shot his revolver into the air to disperse the crowd, but he gave no order to seize Glazman.

He called in the representatives of the U.P.O. and convinced them that Glazman ought to go voluntarily to Resza. Otherwise the ghetto police would lose face; he threatened that he and Dessler would leave the ghetto and let the Germans take over.

The U.P.O. gave in. Glazman left the ghetto for Resza under Gens's personal warranty for his safety.

Gens was enraged at the U.P.O.'s open flouting of his authority and even more furious at the ineffectiveness of his own police. He suspected some of them had connived at the assault on the escort. He instituted a purge of the police force, directed mainly at those Revisionists who he felt had betrayed him by joining the U.P.O. Some were degraded in rank, others sent out of the ghetto to hard labor in nearby quarries. He could not discharge some of his police; they were Gestapo agents. He called one in and said, "I know you're working with Them. What are you doing? Do you think they'll give you a certificate? They'll let you live? Get out of here!" Gens's anger took in other communal officials: teachers, clerks, and administrators were removed from their posts.

The factories were busy, but the Jews no longer believed in a stabilized ghetto. Too many rumors of an impending liquidation were flying around among the Poles and Lithuanians who worked with the Jewish brigades outside the ghetto. Franz Murer was sent to the Eastern Front and in his place came Kittel, a man with a reputation as the liquidator of ghettos. The Glazman affair and the subsequent administrative shake-up indicated to the Jews that not even Gens was certain of the future.

Gens felt his authority weakening. The Germans requested fifty workers for a special project. Before complying with the request, Gens contacted the U.P.O. to ask that they not interfere with him. The U.P.O. replied that what he did was his own business and that the U.P.O. was concerned only with what would happen if the ghetto were ordered liquidated. Gens went to Hingst and described the unrest in the ghetto. Hingst said the Jews had nothing to fear; their labor was needed by the Reich.

Then came the "Vittenberg days." Vittenberg as commander of the U.P.O. was the delegate of that body to the united Polish-Lithuanian resistance committee in the city, headed by Witas, who had been a municipal councilman under the Soviet rule. On July 9, 1943, Witas and Kozlowski, a Communist Party activist, were arrested by the Gestapo. Witas hung himself in prison rather than give out the names of his comrades. Kozlowski gave in after two days of torture. Kittel came to the ghetto and demanded Vittenberg, whom he called the leader of 500 armed Jews. He was told Vittenberg was dead and was shown a false death certificate. A policeman named Averbuch was arrested and released a few hours later. The ghetto saw in this a strategem to delude the Jews into thinking that the Gestapo was merely conducting an investigation.

Late at night on July 15, Gens called the leaders of the U.P.O. to an urgent meeting. Vittenberg, Kovner, Chwojnik, and Chiene Borowska came. Dessler, who was present also, left the room and soon returned with several Lithuanian policemen who grabbed Vittenberg and began dragging him to the ghetto gate. The U.P.O., nervous about the meeting, had already been mobilized. They attacked and beat the police and rescued Vittenberg. The next night Gens stood on the balcony of the administration building and announced to the assembled men, "The Gestapo is demanding that Vittenberg be surrendered to them alive within a few hours. If he is not surrendered, then German tanks and planes will demolish the ghetto by bombing. . . . What's to be done now? Shall we become victims because of one man? Or shall we give up this one and save all?"

The crowd yelled, "Give up Vittenberg! Save the ghetto!"

"Vittenberg is in hiding. Seek him out! Find him!" shouted Gens.

The police and a special force armed with sticks and clubs set out at once. They attacked a house reputed to be U.P.O. headquarters. A policeman fired a shot. The house was empty but at the sound of the shot a wild panic seized the ghetto. Some ran to their malinas crying, "The last hours of the ghetto have arrived!" Others screamed, "For one man should the ghetto be destroyed?" and joined the searchers. Indeed, the war news had been good. The Germans were retreating from the Eastern Front, Italy had capitulated—only a few days, a few weeks, a couple of months, and the war would be over. If the ghetto could only hold out until then!

Gens exhorted the people to search for Vittenberg. He said,

We have set up workshops for you which are economically important to the Germans. . . . You have been given a chance to work and live in peace—and work is our guarantee of staying alive. As for those gangsters, not only do they take no part in all of this, they even try to keep us from doing our jobs. They have separated themselves from the community, trying to force us to do things that will be the end of us. We must stamp them out. We must not feel sorry for them, just as they don't care about us, our wives, and our children. Help us to wipe them out because your lives are at stake. All the Gestapo wants is the life of one man. Just as soon as we hand him over, we'll have peace again in the ghetto. But if we don't do as they ask, it will all be up with us. . . .

The U.P.O. staff faced a dilemma: to turn over their commander or take on itself the responsibility for the loss of thousands of Jewish lives. Without popular support no armed resistance was possible, and the mood of the masses was definitely against Vittenberg. The staff decided to have him surrender. Two of his comrades, Sonia Madejska and Nisl Reznik, knew his hideout. They went to him and reported the staff decision. Vittenberg refused to accept it and fled to another hiding place. A group of old acquaintances found him and told him that Gens and Dessler had guaranteed that he would return unharmed from the hands of the Gestapo. Vittenberg would not listen to them.

A short while later the ghetto police caught him disguised as a woman. He broke away from them and ran into a nearby house. The U.P.O. sent Sonia Madejska, Aba Kovner, and Joseph Glazman (now back in the ghetto) to tell him the staff decision had been unanimous. They repeated Gens's and Dessler's assurances and added that Gens had said he would spend every cent in the treasury to ransom him. Vittenberg again refused to go, saying that the ghetto was on the verge of liquidation and that the Germans wanted to start by destroying the leaders of the resistance.

His comrades agreed with his estimate of the situation but said the ghetto masses were so frightened they could not be reasoned with. If the U.P.O. began to fight now, they would be fighting their Jewish brothers rather than the German enemy. Vittenberg said he would commit suicide. The U.P.O. reported his decision to Gens and Dessler. Gens secretly desired a dead Vittenberg; alive, under torture by the Germans he might say too much. Had Vittenberg committed suicide without asking him first, Gens would have had no problem. But Gens had to play the role forced on him by the Germans; furthermore, Dessler, whom he distrusted, was present. He said no: the Germans wanted Vittenberg alive. Vittenberg finally gave in to the pleadings of his comrades and was escorted by the ghetto police to a waiting Gestapo automobile. The next morning he was found dead in the courtyard of the Gestapo headquarters, his hair burned, his eyes pierced, and his broken arms tied behind his back.

The U.P.O. was now out in the open. It feared new demands from the Germans and it knew it had no support from the masses. Its members prepared to leave the ghetto. On July 22, a group of twenty armed men led by Joseph Glazman left the ghetto gate posing as a column of workers. The group fell into a German ambush in the forest; they fought desperately but only a few finally got away.

The next day Neugebauer came to Gens with the leaden dog-tags found on the corpses and from the files learned their names. He applied the principle of collective responsibility: their families and the brigade foremen to whose units they had been attached were shot. Gens dictated an editorial for the *Ghetto News,* in which he said, "This spilled blood should be our last warning. We should remember that there's no other path than the path of work for us. . . ."

The Jews no longer believed his assurances that the ghetto would not be destroyed nor that their labor would save them. "Malinas!" was the cry of the day. Underground tunnels were dug to the "Aryan" side, one such being a very large one that reached from the Jewish hospital to the vicinity of the railroad station. Jews began to disappear one by one, discarding the yellow badge when they got into the city, melting away in the general population, finding hiding places with friendly Christians, old neighbors, or political comrades.

On August 1 the work brigades returning to the ghetto brought word that they had all been discharged from their jobs. The alarm spread—"The Germans don't need our labor any more!" and its implication—"We are doomed to death!" A few work units were reemployed; the rest clamored for Gens to help them.

A few days later came the order for those wanting to work at the railroad station or at the airdrome under construction to register for work. There was a rush to get work permits at the Labor Office. On August 6 the work columns were all diverted to the railroad station where trains were already waiting for them. "Ponary!" went up the cry. A battle broke out between the armed SS guards and the unarmed workers. Three hundred were killed, some escaped to run back into the ghetto, and the rest were packed into the trains. Gens came to the trains with bread and water for the deportees and news that they were not going to Ponary but to a labor camp in Estonia. He told them their women and children would soon follow them. The transport was short of its quota, so the Germans rounded up workers from other units in the city until the full number had been reached—1,000 in all.

The first letter came from Estonia a week later. The workers were indeed in a labor camp. Gens then said in a speech that the Germans had been for months demanding that he send workers to camps in Riga and Estonia. He had kept putting them off and that was why they took the workers so suddenly by subterfuge. "Be calm. Go to work. All is well."

Men and women went to work uneasy in their minds. Not all went to work: a group of fifty U.P.O. men and women left the ghetto to join the partisans. More letters came from Estonia—and indecision mounted. Some said the camps were only eighty kilometers from the Russian front; escape by bribery might be possible. Vilna was doomed anyway—then why not answer the call for volunteers for Estonia? Others said that the camps were only a stopping place for another Ponary, that the Germans could not be trusted, that the letters were forgeries.

Relatives and families of the first deportees were the first to be asked to register, and left for Estonia. Those who did not sign up were politely asked to do so. When they failed to show up at the ghetto gate to be brought to the trains, the Jewish police hunted for them and dragged them away by force from their homes or malinas. Gens ordered the police to make sure that each train had the required number. If not, the police themselves would make up the quota. The early days of snatching reappeared, but this time it was the Jewish police who did the snatching. Trains left daily for Estonia from the 19th to the 24th of August.

Gens, still clinging to the idea that he could maintain a work ghetto, began checking on what empty buildings could be used for new factories.

His mother, whose apartment was upstairs from his in the ghetto, asked him, the question probably the result of instigation by fearful neighbors, "Is it true what I've heard? That you and your friends, about 2,000 in all, will soon depart and leave the rest of us to calamity and destruction?" His answer was, "We're all staying here. Don't spread unrest. It's dangerous. Those who have run away were cowards and fell into trouble. That's what happened to the twenty big-shots who were captured by two Gentiles. What good did the weapons in their hands do them? We must wait patiently. The end is in sight. Meanwhile the deportations for labor camps are suspended. If They want only workers, then those not absolutely necessary for Them will be shot. Therefore, we must be a community of workers and then we'll be saved."

On the first of September mass deportations were ordered. The Lithuanian auxiliaries were withdrawn and Estonian detachments appeared in the ghetto, ostensibly to aid in the deportations. They were brutal and savage. Gens objected to their presence and asked that they be withdrawn. He said the Jewish police would do whatever was ordered. "We don't need outsiders."

In keeping with his policy, Gens sent older men and women to the trains, but Kittel turned them back. Many regarded that as proof that the Germans wanted only good workers for their camps. The U.P.O. issued a proclamation calling for an armed revolt against the Germans. It set up barricades in several streets, but the German and Estonian troops sent in to speed up the deportations were too strongly armed to be held back by the ghetto fighters. The Germans blew up a few buildings and went on with their main task, almost as though they were brushing away flies. Fighting went on sporadically during the day; at night, when the Germans withdrew from the ghetto, most of the U.P.O. members left the ghetto by various means, including the sewers, to join their comrades in the nearby Rudnicki and Narocz forests.

The deportations lasted for three days. On the fifth of September, Gens announced that no more transports would leave for Estonia. Exactly 7,130 had been deported; 1,000 more were resettled in the Kailis fur plant in the city and another 1,000 in the H.F.K. center, a German work area, leaving about 8,000 in the ghetto. Brigades for work in the city were terminated; Jews could work henceforth only in factories inside the ghetto.

The factories reopened. The Jews drew a deep breath. Maybe this time Gens was right. New orders were received from the Wehrmacht; a represenative of the big Todt firm came to discuss the formation of a plant to make tinware. The few remaining U.P.O. members saw that resistance in the ghetto had no hope of success; they filtered across the city into the forests.

Dessler, perhaps as a provocatory act, asked Gens if he would run away if he knew the ghetto was to be entirely liquidated. Mrs. Gens, who was present, paled at the question. She said she hoped her husband would agree to leave, but he pondered only a moment before answering, "No. My people come before my family."

On September 13, 1943, Martin Weiss, an officer who had no use for Jews but who liked Gens, warned him that he was on the list of those to be executed. He advised him to disappear. Gens replied, "No. If I, the Chief of the Ghetto, run away, thousands of Jews will pay with their lives for my desertion."

The following day Neugebauer called Gens to Gestapo headquarters. He was accused of aiding the partisans and was shot on the spot.

The Vilna Ghetto was finally liquidated nine days later, on September 23, 1943. The older men and women were sent to be shot at Ponary, about 5,000 were sent to the death camp at Majdanek, and the remainder sent to labor camps.

11

Gen's death had little impact on the ghetto. By the time he was killed, his title was meaningless, his power nonexistent. Some called him a martyr for the Jewish people; others saw in his end retribution for his villanies. It must be remembered that most of the diaries and memoirs of that period were written by individuals biased in their views (Bundists, anti-Revisionists, anti-Lithuanians, and intellectuals who looked down on Gens as a Lithuanian soldier). Nevertheless, no one accused him of megalomania or corruption. Representative comments were:

> *Szmerke Kaczerginski, a poet and partisan fighter:* Gens knew that the slaughter was spreading in Byelorussia and that the goal of the Germans was to exterminate us root and branch. He thought he'd succeed in freeing some of the inhabitants of the ghetto. He played for time, waiting for the front to get so close that the Germans could not carry out their malignant purpose. He believed Murer and Weiss. The two knaves assured Gens that the Vilna Ghetto would not be liquidated. Gens believed them and so he persuaded the masses they should work hard because the ghetto was founded on work. . . . Gens did not understand he was only a tool in the hands of the Gestapo and that, wanting to help the Jews, he actually helped the Germans in their diabolical work. . . .

Isaac Kowalski, printer: Gens applied his own laws and collaborated with the bloody Germans. At a later date he . . .
paid for his Jewishness with his life.

Zelig Kalmanovich, literary critic: Gens was a very weak man, easily swayed. While he spoke to our people [the Resistance] he
was wholeheartedly with us. He wanted earnestly to help and
he did help. But as soon as Dessler started to work on him,
Gens changed. He didn't remember what he'd told us and
would do the exact opposite."

Masha Rolnik, a fifteen-year-old girl, in her diary: They said he'd
been executed, nobody knew where, but they said it was not
at Ponary. Nobody was sorry for him, except maybe the
policemen. . . . everyone repeats the same thing: the Hitlerites
would never let any accomplice or witnesses of their deeds
live. It is a fact that he was a real collaborator. Otherwise They
wouldn't have confided in him or let him bear arms. He
wouldn't have had special privileges. . . . Our first-floor
neighbor says that if Gens had not fooled people with his
assurances that by obedience they could escape Ponary and
await liberation and also that resisting the Germans would
come to naught, then the ghetto people would probably have
been more successful in saving themselves and joining the partisans in the forest. . . . although he served the occupying
forces with devotion, he did not escape the death common
to all. . . .

An anonymous survivor, as reported by Leizer Ran, a journalist: The
Jews wanted to see in Gens a *Rosh ha-Ghetto,* a leader who
would have their whole interest at heart. It's no wonder that
they chewed and rechewed every least action in their behalf
and held it like an ointment to their bleeding wounds. Unfortunately, from the visible facts, that image of him was
drowned in the stream of constantly flowing Jewish blood.

Abraham Ajzen, labor journalist: The majority of the people had a sound social instinct. They did not regard him as their true representative. The thousands of slaves who worked day in and day out at hard labor in the brigades, the hundreds of families whose members were beaten by his police, those flogged or surrendered to the Germans on command—none of these felt he represented them. And of course, the underground organization couldn't regard him as such while they prepared for battle with the Germans. . . . He gave the Gestapo the asked-for quota of victims but to the very end he kept his word and never gave them the children. . . .

12

Jacob Gens was a man of great complexity. In spite of his disclaimer that he was no dreamer, he had always been a man with noble ideals—ideals of a free and independent Lithuania, ideals of a Palestine conquered by the Jews to be their national homeland. He saw no contradiction between the two. While the Jews were in the Diaspora they should be strong supporters of the nations that sheltered them, not separatists demanding special privileges nor cosmopolitans denying patriotic bonds. At the same time Jews should prepare themselves to fight and take over the only place to which they had historic rights—the land of Israel. Yet he was a very practical idealist, willing to make immediate compromises in the interest of a future goal.

Without illusions about the German hatred for the Jews, he nevertheless clung to the illusion that he could minimize the result of that hatred. If the Germans wanted a quota of Jews for killing, he would supply that quota and thereby save the rest of the Jews. If the Germans needed skilled workers for their war production, he would give them such workers and thereby save the economically useless (to the Germans) members of their families. His aim was to keep the entire mass of the Jews under his control, to keep them by petty propitiations from being wholly annihilated. Gens's idealism permeated the ghetto and helped to prevent the bitterness of class hatred that prevailed in Warsaw and the apathy that characterized Lodz. Gens set the moral tone for the ghetto and made it a place where no one informed on pregnant women, on doctors treating contagious diseases, or on official and unofficial smuggling. He was never accused of seeing himself as a Tsar or a Führer. He was incorruptible and the example of his incorruptibility was ever present before the police. They were neither bribe-takers nor influence-peddlers, as were the police of Warsaw and Lodz.

Gens expressed his viewpoint well when he said that the ghetto was like a Death Row with the condemned placed in full view of the execution chamber and that his purpose was to postpone the fatal day. Unlike Czerniakow, therefore, to save many he cooperated in the killing of a few. His show of independence was greater than Rumkowski's, yet in the long run he too was manipulated like a puppet by the Germans. His strong hand and iron discipline discouraged the corruption that ate at the ghettos of Warsaw and Lodz, yet his strength was at the beck and call of the Germans.

In the end he realized he had been only a tool, that he had succeeded in nothing but facilitating the extermination of the very Jews he wanted to save, that he was a failure in his own eyes and in the eyes of those who had looked up to him and trusted him as a crafty warrior against the murderers.

Was that why he went so willingly to Gestapo headquarters on that last day, in full awareness of his doom?

Afterword and Opinion

In Treblinka bin ich nit geven. . . .
                                    H. LEIVICK

One fact must not be forgotten in any discussion of the period of the Holocaust, and that is that the Germans had a plan for "the final solution of the Jewish question." The solution was extermination. The Germans had no desire to use the Jews as slaves or unpaid laborers, no desire to herd them in reservations where they would live or die remote from "Aryans," no desire to repeat history by forced conversions or expulsions. They wanted a real final solution: the wiping out of the Jews, root and branch.

That final solution must always be kept in mind in evaluating the role of the Judenräte and their leaders. The Judenrat was *not* a Kehillah, a Jewish Community Council concerned with specific religious and social activities of the Jews. A Judenrat was set up by the Germans for one purpose and one purpose only: to see that German orders were carried out with dispatch. Whatever else the Judenrat did was of no importance to the conquerors, no matter how essential to Jewish survival, as long as those concomitant undertakings did not interfere with the punctual and full execution of official commands. Those other undertakings were tolerated, sometimes encouraged, they helped to build up illusions and to conceal from the Jews the already decided "final solution" of the Jewish problem, but they had nothing to do with the primary function of the Judenrat.

Dr. Isaiah Trunk, the historian who has made tue most complete study of the Jewish Councils of Eastern Europe, has said:

> The tasks of the Councils can be divided into three classes (1) those imposed by the authorities, such as conduct of the census of the Jewish population, the supply of forced labor, registration of candidates for the work camps, for deportation, etc. (2) routine tasks in social welfare, medical care, and in the economic and cultural fields—tasks which were, in the main, a continuation of prewar activities; (3) new tasks made essential by the complete elimination of the Jewish population . . . from governmental and municipal services, such as food supplies, the management of the ghetto dwellings, industry, health, police and judicial services, etc. . . .

Only the first task was obligatory, imposed by the Germans. The others were undertaken voluntarily.

Keeping the primary function of the Councils in mind, the question then arises whether the other two functions hastened or slowed the pace of the German extermination program. The answer is written in fire and ashes. German science and efficiency were such that the extermination program went rolling on, totally independent of war needs and equally totally independent of anything done by the Councils or by Jews as individuals. Then how can we understand the actions of Gens, Czerniakow, and Rumkowski in that time of terror? Were they stupid? Ambitious? Collaborators? Seekers after martyrdom? Misguided altruists?

The wages of stupidity, like sin, is death. But can a man who is ignorant be called stupid? Then are we all stupid, ignorant as we are individually and collectively of our future. Rumkowski certainly never knew that at Chelmno there existed a death camp. He may have expected that no good awaited the deportees, but that "no good" probably meant to him starvation and disease and even "death from natural causes." Yet were that "no good" as he surmised, there was still a chance for some Jews to survive. In Lodz itself during the existence of the ghetto the Germans engaged in no pogroms, in no senseless arbitrary murders. He had no reason to believe that the Germans had planned an extermination process more efficient than wanton killing. In Warsaw Czerniakow saw in the intemperate slaughter of individuals and the systematic starvation of the ghetto as a whole evidence of Nazi viciousness, not the preliminaries to wholesale butchery. When he realized what lay in store for the Jews of Warsaw, he killed himself. Gens was fully aware of how low in the scale of the animal kingdom the Germans regarded the Jews. From the very first days of the occupation, Jews were killed en masse as though they were vermin. Nevertheless, he too could not bring himself to a belief that the Germans would sacrifice their hope of world conquest in order to make a Europe literally *Judenrein*.

1

All three were cursed with a knowledge of Jewish history. All three believed in the fiction that man can learn from history, and not in the facts: that the running water in the stream is never the same, that no present mimics the past, that experience is no warranty of success. They forgot that the race is not always to the swift nor the battle to the strong nor comprehension to the clever. Hitlerism was not merely fascism but fascism *cum* racist genocide of a kind never before encountered in history. Even Czerniakow, who had read *The Forty Days of Musa Dagh*, could find no parallel. The slaughter of the Armenians was not comparable; it was not carried out by a high-minded, civilized nation on ideological "scientific" grounds. All three men knew of the bloody Crusades, of the fiery Inquisition, of the soul-destroying medieval ghettos and the Tsarist pogroms. And all three believed that modern civilization would not tolerate a return to the dark days of the past. True, ghettos were established, but the ghetto could only be a transitional stage (if Germany were ultimately victorious, an outcome in which none of them put credence) to the expulsion of the Jews or their resettlement on tracts of land like those of the American Indians. They, no more than the rest of the world, believed that Hitler meant what he said, when he declared that whether Germany won or lost the war, one thing was certain—no Jews would survive.

Collaborators they were not. A collaborator with the Nazis worked with them out of ideological conviction or out of a desire for power or riches or simply to save his own skin. Rumkowski, Czerniakow, and Gens were not collaborators in any sense of the word. What they did may have helped the Germans, but that was not their aim. Not one of them profited by his deeds, and by profiting I do not mean in cash but in the most precious possession of all—in life itself. Czerniakow could have gone to Palestine, yet he refused to leave and ended by taking his own life. Rumkowski could have stayed behind in Lodz to eventually be liberated by the Russians, yet he chose to go with "his Jews" to Auschwitz. Gens certainly was warned of his impending death and had connections good enough to warrant his safety, yet he went to be shot in the courtyard of the Gestapo headquarters.

Then were they seekers after martyrdom, willingly surrendering their earthly lives for a more enduring celestial crown? Did they feel that *Kiddush ha-Shem,* the Sanctification of the Name, transcended all mundane considerations? Not at all. Czerniakow was thoroughly secular, an outward conformer but not a believer in religion. Rumkowski was superficially sentimental about Jewish beliefs and customs but by no means averse to discarding them when he felt that action necessary. Gens was a Jewish nationalist who regarded Judaism as merely one strand in the fabric of Jewish life.

All three were ambitious men, ambitious in a very special way, in a way bound up with an altruism amazing under the circumstances. They all wanted to save the Jews and, not at all inciden-

tally, to cover themselves with glory. Rumkowski was the most bla-
tant in his ambition. He wanted to go down in history as the savior
of the Jews, not as a Don Isaac Abrabanel or a Josef Süss
Oppenheim or even as a Moses leading his people to a Promised
Land but as the savior of the Jews in their own homes. To that
end he established his archives. To that end he built up his
"productive ghetto" to prove to the Germans the economic value
of the Jews that they might be saved from destruction. To that
end he gave up unproductive elements: dispirited and antagonis-
tic Jews, old men and women, the sick, and eventually the young
children he loved so much.

Czerniakow, too, was ambitious, but in a quieter way. He
enjoyed praise and was annoyed by criticism, but neither praise
nor criticism kept him from doing what he thought was essential
for the survival of the Jews. He, too, saw himself, as he said, in
a historic role. He felt that his position in that role would be honored by worldwide Jewry in the days to come. He saw his task
as one of overcoming the confused and imposed irrationality of
life in the ghetto, of overcoming it by a calm and methodical
application of sound business principles. Once the economic bur-
dens of the ghetto were lightened, then it could go on its way
to build a new life, like the medieval ghettos of history. Meanwhile, his attitude was one of accommodation: I will bend my
head before the storm, I will obey the evil decrees, I will not anger
the enemy. I don't have to run to help the Germans, like Rumkowski; I don't have to curry favor by informing on fellow Jews,
like Kohn and Heller; I don't have to plan for a hopeless resistance, like the Anti-Fascist Bloc. If I can only mitigate their troubles now, then the Jews will survive, and future generations will
applaud me as a farsighted leader.

Ambition to be known as the savior of the Jews or as their guide
through the wilderness of Nazi bestiality was not in Gens's mind.
He was a thoroughgoing idealist. His ambition was to preserve
the Jews as a nation. He believed he could reach that goal by a
combination of accommodation and resistance. He believed in a
"productive ghetto" for the same reasons Rumkowski did—to

show the Germans how necessary the Jews were for the war effort. He believed in the punctilious following of German orders as Czerniakow did, lest there be a return to the days of the wholesale massacres at Ponary. Yet he also believed in resistance to those same orders wherever practical, using bribery, chicanery, and smuggling to evade them. He kept from the hands of the executioners those in whom he felt lay the future of the Jewish people, the children. Those he would not sacrifice, as Rumkowski did, for the sake of a productive ghetto. He never doubted that the Germans would lose the war. And he never doubted that he would be blamed for helping them. Nevertheless, when that happened, once the truth was known he would be hailed as the energetic leader unscrupulous (in the positive sense of the word) in his efforts to preserve the Jews as a people.

2

All three men combined altruism and ambition with a very special concept ingrained in their Jewishness. That concept, although none of them expressed it as such, was *tsedekah,* a Hebrew word poorly and variously translated as righteousness, benevolence, love of one's fellow-man, *caritas,* faithfulness to mankind. *Tsedekah* is a concise way of saying, "No man is an island," of "He who saves one life is as one who saves the whole world," of "Love one another." *Tsedekah* is immanent in Jewishness. It had its origins in the words of the prophets, it was elaborated in Talmudic literature, it developed throughout the course of Jewish history. *Tsedekah* is in the blood, bone, and flesh of the Jews, not because they are a more moral or a more ethical people than others but because history made *tsedekah* necessary. From Haman to the Crusaders to Torquemada to the Black Hundreds, Jews had collective responsibility. Accusations of treason, ritual murder, and well-poisoning bound them together. "A Jew is beaten in Algeria and the Jews of Virginia protest," commented one observer. "There but for the grace of God go I" is as much a part of Jewish thought as "Hear, O Israel, the Lord thy God, the Lord is One." *Tsedekah* made the Jews philanthropists, promoters of agricultural settlements in Argentina, ransomers of slaves from the Turks, Court Jews—and Judenrat leaders.

Before the war and the occupation, Rumkowski showed the workings of *tsedekah* in his labors for the orphans, Czerniakow in his efforts to alleviate the effects of the anti-Semitic laws against craftsmen, Gens paradoxically both in his Lithuanian patriotism and in the military training which he felt was necessary to ensure Palestine as the eventual homeland of the Jews. It was *tsedekah* that made the proud Czerniakow submit to the humiliations of the Germans and the contumely of his fellow-Jews, *tsedekah* that had the arrogant Rumkowski running to beg favors from Biebow, *tsedekah* that showed Gens the way out of the moral dilemma before him in the cases of the partisans and Vittenberg. It was *tsedekah*, finally, that brought them to their deaths.

But, as Merleau-Ponty has said, "He who acts morally becomes immoral as soon as he loses regard for the nature of his acts." *Tsedekah* was, alas!, not the only source of their actions. Rumkowski and Gens combined *tsedekah* with hubris, a staunch belief that what they did was right, and therefore a willingness to play God in deciding who was to live and who was to die. Czerniakow, by killing himself, abdicated rather than take on that divine role. His deed was a negative one, no answer at all. Rumkowski chose the very young and the old to propitiate the German Moloch in order to maintain his "productive ghetto." Gens participated in the gathering of the bloody quotas so that the German fury would not consume all.

The making of such a bitter choice, of deciding on death or life, was nothing new in Jewish history. Maimonides' ruling, quoted by the rabbis to Gens, was not looked on as binding. In 1827, Tsar Nicholas I ordered the Jewish communities of Russia to deliver quotas of Jewish males from the ages of twelve to twenty-five to the army for a twenty-five-year term of service. Penalties for nonconformance were heavy fines and/or the conscription of the community leaders. Exempted were the wealthy merchants, rabbis, *gymnasium* graduates, licensed skilled workers, and farm laborers. Catch-22 was that the number of the last three categories was trivial and the first two, limited. The communities, forced to choose, rejected Maimonides' advice and themselves decided who were expendable. They selected not the clever scholars, not the boys with "sharp heads," but the dull and ignorant. By giving up the latter, the leaders hoped to save those who would be the sages of the future. How much different from them were Gens and Rumkowski?

3

All three were men in charge of a sinking boat and they did not know its sinking was inevitable, riddled as its bottom was by German hatred and perfidy. They believed that by jettisoning some of the human cargo the boat would be lightened enough for them to bring it to a safe port. They violated Kant's categorical imperative: "Act so that in your person as well as the person of every other man you are treating mankind as an end, not as a means." Their end was not the preservation of Jews, but the preservation of the Jewish people. To that end they took the wrong path.

We can say of them—"They meant well."

We can also say of them justifiably, I believe—"They did the best they could." They acted. Right or wrong, they acted. To them applies Karl Jaspers' statement: "The man who will not act or speak except in total righteousness achieves nothing . . . the man who seeks to be true must run the risk of being mistaken, of putting himself in the wrong. . . ." Then indeed they can be honored for their intentions.

I have ended with an apology for men whose names have become a hissing and a byword in the history of the Holocaust. Why not? Is it for us to judge them, we who were not there? Smugness and afterwit do not become us. In another time, in another place, could or would the noblest of us have done otherwise?

Selected Bibliography

General

Raul Hilberg: *The Destruction of European Jewry*, Chicago, 1961.
Isaiah Trunk: *Judenrat*, New York, 1972.

Lodz

A. Eisenbach (editor): *Documents and Materials from the Period of the German Occupation of Poland*, Warsaw, 1946 (Polish).
Shlomo Frank: *Diary of the Lodz Ghetto*, Tel Aviv, 1958 (Yiddish).
I. Wolf Jasny: *The History of the Jews in Lodz in the Years of the German Extermination of the Jews* (two volumes), Tel Aviv, 1960, 1969 (Yiddish).
David Sierakowiak: *Diary*, Warsaw, 1960 (Polish).
Israel Tabaksblat: *The Destruction of Lodz*, Buenos Aires, 1946 (Yiddish).
Isaiah Trunk: *The Ghetto of Lodz*, New York, 1962 (Yiddish).

209

WARSAW

Mary Berg: *Warsaw Ghetto,* New York, 1945.
Adam Czerniakow: *Warsaw Ghetto Diary,* Jerusalem, 1968 (Hebrew).
Ludwik Hirszfeld: *The Story of One Man's Life,* Warsaw, 1946 (Polish).
Chaim Kaplan: *Scroll of Agony* (translated and edited by Abraham I. Katsh), New York, 1965.
Emanuel Ringelblum: *Notes from the Warsaw Ghetto* (translated and edited by Jacob Sloan), New York, 1958.
Noëmi Szac-Wajnkranc: *Lost in the Flames,* Warsaw, 1950 (Polish).
Jonas Turkow: *This Is the Way It Was,* Buenos Aires, 1948 (Yiddish).
Leonard Tushnet: *The Uses of Adversity,* New York, 1966.
Michael Zylberberg: *A Warsaw Diary,* London, 1969.

VILNA

Mendl Balberishki: *Stronger than Iron,* Tel Aviv, 1967 (Yiddish).
Mark Dworzhetski: *Jerusalem of Lithuania in Battle and Downfall,* Paris, 1948 (Yiddish).
V. Grodzenskis (editor): *Documents Accuse,* Vilnius, 1971.
Herman Kruk: *Diary of the Vilna Ghetto,* New York, 1961 (Yiddish).
Moishe Shutan: *Ghetto and Forest,* Tel Aviv, 1971 (Yiddish).

A note on names: The names of persons and places have been left almost always as they appear in the original documents, but some place names have been changed to the more familiar or Anglicized forms (e.g., Warsaw for Warszawa, Vilna for Vilnius or Wilno, Auschwitz for Oswiecim, etc.). *Kehillah* has been used throughout instead of the official but unfamiliar *Gmina Zydowska.*